Doing What Works

10 Common-Sense Leadership Practices to Improve Student Learning

Chris Weber

Solution Tree | Press

Copyright © 2020 by Solution Tree Press

Materials appearing here are copyrighted. With one exception, all rights are reserved. Readers may reproduce only those pages marked "Reproducible." Otherwise, no part of this book may be reproduced or transmitted in any form or by any means (electronic, photocopying, recording, or otherwise) without prior written permission of the publisher.

555 North Morton Street
Bloomington, IN 47404
800.733.6786 (toll free) / 812.336.7700
FAX: 812.336.7790

email: info@SolutionTree.com
SolutionTree.com

Visit **go.SolutionTree.com/leadership** to download the free reproducibles in this book.

Printed in the United States of America

Library of Congress Cataloging-in-Publication Data

Names: Weber, Chris (Chris A.), author.
Title: Doing what works : ten common-sense leadership practices to improve
   student learning / Chris Weber.
Description: Bloomington, IN : Solution Tree Press, 2020. | Includes
   bibliographical references and index.
Identifiers: LCCN 2019013126 | ISBN 9781949539196
Subjects: LCSH: Education--Aims and objectives--United States. | Effective
   teaching--United States. | Academic achievement--United States.
Classification: LCC LA217.2 .W44 2020 | DDC 370.11--dc23
LC record available at https://lccn.loc.gov/2019013126

Solution Tree
Jeffrey C. Jones, CEO
Edmund M. Ackerman, President

Solution Tree Press
President and Publisher: Douglas M. Rife
Associate Publisher: Sarah Payne-Mills
Art Director: Rian Anderson
Managing Production Editor: Kendra Slayton
Production Editor: Alissa Voss
Content Development Specialist: Amy Rubenstein
Copy Editor: Jessi Finn
Proofreader: Elisabeth Abrams
Text and Cover Designer: Abigail Bowen
Editorial Assistant: Sarah Ludwig

I dedicate this book to Captain Gregg "Butch" Lewis
(1970–1989), USAF, USAFA Class of 1992—
the finest man I've ever known—and to the educators
of Irvine Unified School District.

—Chris Weber

Acknowledgments

This is my ninth book with Solution Tree, and I have found there is no better partner for an author or consultant than this company. I believe Solution Tree, guided by Jeff Jones, is the preeminent educational publishing and professional development company in the world. There is no finer man or publisher than Solution Tree Press president, Douglas Rife, and I thank him for a decade of support. Thanks to Alissa Voss for her outstanding support in editing this book; no one supports an author in creating a book better than Solution Tree. I cannot thank enough the professional development and events departments at Solution Tree, led by Shannon Ritz and Renee Marshall, for supporting me and others as we share our passion and ideas with colleagues around the world. I hope this book moves Solution Tree one step closer to achieving its vision of transforming education worldwide.

Thanks to my friends, coauthors, and colleagues Mike Mattos, Austin Buffum, Janet Malone, and Laurie Robinson for guiding me so patiently and wisely in my professional journey. Finally, I believe that Rick and Becky DuFour were the most innovative, transformational, and significant educators in the United States since Benjamin Bloom; I miss them, and we honor their work. Every idea within this book rests on the foundation of Professional Learning Communities at Work™, and no practice within this book will be successful or sustained without a collaborative commitment to all students by all staff. I look forward to a day when PLCs are not something we do but simply who we are.

—Chris Weber

Solution Tree Press would like to thank the following reviewers:

Joanna Ayers
Instructional Coach
Clinton Middle School
Clinton, Iowa

Chris Chappotin
Principal
STEAM Middle School
Burleson, Texas

Louis Lim
Vice Principal
Richmond Green Secondary School
Richmond Hill, Ontario, Canada

Kelli McCord
Instructional Coach
Marble Falls High School
Marble Falls, Texas

Jason Ozbolt
Dean of Students
Lockport Township High School
Lockport, Illinois

Mary Beth Riley
Principal
Maple Glen Elementary School
Westfield, Indiana

Amber Webb
Stage I Teacher
The Roeper School
Bloomfield Hills, Michigan

Visit **go.SolutionTree.com/leadership** to download the free reproducibles in this book.

Table of Contents

Reproducible pages are in italics.

About the Author xi

Introduction 1
    The Reality of Initiative Fatigue. 4
    The Groundwork for Success: PLC at Work 5
    The Power to Effect Change 7
    The Ten Common-Sense Leadership Practices. 8

Chapter 1
Teaching Less so Students Learn More 15
    Educational Practices That Defy Common Sense 16
    Research-Based Best Practices in Education 17
    Strategies and Insights for Improving Student Learning 20
    Conclusion. 27
    Next Steps. 28

Chapter 2
Predicting and Preventing Challenges 31
    Educational Practices That Defy Common Sense 32
    Research-Based Best Practices in Education 33
    Strategies and Insights for Improving Student Learning 34
    Conclusion. 43
    Next Steps. 44

Chapter 3
Letting Students Do the Talking and the Learning 47
    Educational Practices That Defy Common Sense 48
    Research-Based Best Practices in Education 49

Strategies and Insights for Improving
　　Student Learning 50
Conclusion... 56
Next Steps.. 57

Chapter 4
Keeping Learning Targets Visible and Still 59
Educational Practices That Defy Common Sense 60
Research-Based Best Practices in Education 60
Strategies and Insights for Improving Student Learning 62
Conclusion... 68
Next Steps.. 70

Chapter 5
Nurturing Behavioral Habits That Affect Motivation 73
Educational Practices That Defy Common Sense 74
Research-Based Best Practices in Education 75
Strategies and Insights for Improving Student Learning 80
Conclusion..91
Next Steps.. 92

Chapter 6
Fostering Two-Way Feedback 95
Educational Practices That Defy Common Sense 96
Research-Based Best Practices in Education 97
Strategies and Insights for Improving Student Learning 99
Conclusion.. 106
Next Steps...*107*

Chapter 7
Emphasizing Skills Alongside or Above Content 109
Educational Practices That Defy Common Sense 110
Research-Based Best Practices in Education 111
Strategies and Insights for Improving Student Learning 116
Conclusion...120
Next Steps...*122*

Chapter 8
Promoting Rigorous Learning Tasks 125
    Educational Practices That Defy Common Sense 125

    Research-Based Best Practices in Education 126

    Strategies and Insights for Improving Student Learning 129

    Conclusion..133

    Next Steps..134

Chapter 9
Empowering Parents as Partners in Education 137
    Educational Practices That Defy Common Sense 137

    Research-Based Best Practices in Education 139

    Strategies and Insights for Improving Student Learning 142

    Conclusion..145

    Next Steps..147

Chapter 10
Inspiring and Enabling Staff Engagement 149
    Educational Practices That Defy Common Sense 149

    Research-Based Best Practices in Education 151

    Strategies and Insights for Improving Student Learning 152

    Conclusion...160

    Next Steps..162

Epilogue.. 163

References and Resources........................... 167

Index 183

About the Author

Chris Weber, EdD, is an expert in behavior, mathematics, and response to intervention (RTI) who consults and presents internationally to audiences on important topics in education. As a teacher, principal, and director in California and Illinois, Chris worked with his colleagues to develop RTI systems that have led to high levels of learning at schools across the United States. In addition to writing and consulting, he continues to work in Irvine Unified School District in California, supporting some of the best and highest-performing schools in the country.

Chris has been in service to community and country his entire life. A graduate of the U.S. Air Force Academy, he flew C-141s during his military career. He is also a former high school, middle school, and elementary school teacher and administrator.

To learn more about Chris's work, visit Chris Weber Education (https://chriswebereducation.com) or follow @WeberEducation on Twitter.

To book Chris Weber for professional development, contact pd@SolutionTree.com.

Introduction

Education isn't broken. Richard DuFour (2015) magnificently makes this case in his book *In Praise of American Educators*. DuFour (2015) reports the following.

- High school graduation rates are at an all-time high (*Education Week*, 2014).

- More students are taking advanced placement (AP) courses, and students are passing AP tests at a higher rate (College Board, 2014).

- Student performance on the National Assessment of Educational Progress (NAEP) and the Trends in International Mathematics and Science Study (TIMSS) assessment has steadily improved during the last decade of the 20th century and during the entirety of the 21st century (Mullis, Martin, Foy, & Arora, 2012; Ravitch, 2014).

- While 10 percent of parents report that public schools are failing and 18 percent give public schools grades of A or B, only 1 percent of parents report that their oldest child's school is failing, and 75 percent give their local school a grade of A or B (Phi Delta Kappa, 2014). These are the best local school grades in the history of Phi Delta Kappa's (2014) Polls of the Public's Attitudes Toward the Public Schools.

- Nearly 90 percent of students agree that teacher-student relations are positive, a percentage well above the average of industrialized nations within the Organisation for Economic Co-operation and Development (OECD, 2013).

- When controlling for student poverty, students from the United States rank first in the world on the OECD's Programme for International Student Assessment (PISA; OECD, 2014). When including students living in poverty (and the United States has the highest percentage of students living in poverty among industrialized nations), the United

States scores in the middle of the pack, or just below. (While I include this in a list of educational strengths, I do not mean to suggest that the United States has provided adequate services and supports for students living in poverty; the success is only relative to other nations, and we, as educators and as a society, must continue to better serve all students and eliminate poverty.)

While an educational crisis does not exist, we—educators and educator leaders—can and must improve our practices, approaches, and mindsets regarding who learns at all levels (all students), what is learned, and how learning best occurs. These successes have occurred as substantial changes have affected both our students and the world around them. The characteristics of the students we serve have changed; for example, the number and percent of students living in poverty and speaking a language other than English at home have grown at significant rates (National Center for Education Statistics [NCES], 2019; Suitts, 2015). Additionally, the world for which we prepare students has changed as well. Consider these facts (Carnevale, Smith, & Strohl, 2010, 2012).

- The percentage of jobs that require postsecondary education has increased by 2.3 times since the 1970s, and a college degree is increasingly necessary for access to the middle class.
- Workers who do not graduate from high school, or who graduate unready for college or a skilled career, will be limited to service, sales, and office support jobs—jobs that pay low salaries and that are in decline.

The future for which we are preparing students has changed and continues to change—and education increasingly represents the difference maker in students' success (Bordoff, Furman, & Bendor, 2007). As Edmonds noted in the 1960s and 1970s (Edmonds, 1979), teachers, schools, and education can help students beat the odds. Classes are increasingly fixed. Children born into the lower class are ten times more likely to live in the lower class as adults than children born into the upper class, and children born into the upper class are fourteen times more likely to earn a postsecondary degree than children born into the lower class (Edsall, 2012; Greenstone, Looney, Patashnik, & Yu, 2013).

In a rapidly changing, increasingly global world, we must commit to continuous improvement and to reflection on our current practices. The status quo is simply not an option, even in the highest performing schools. We simply must continue to evolve and improve. That's what professions and professionals do, and education is the most important profession in the world. Regarding continuous improvement, researchers Elizabeth City, Richard Elmore, Sarah Fiarman, and Lee Teitel (2009) state:

> You can raise the level of the content that students are taught. You can increase the skill and knowledge that teachers bring to the teaching of that content. And you can increase the level of students' active learning of the content. . . . If you raise the level of content without changing the level of knowledge and skill that teachers bring to the content, you get what we see with considerable frequency in American classrooms: low-level teaching of high-level content. Teachers assign high-level text or complex problems, and then structure student learning around fill-in-the-blank worksheets, or walk students through a straight procedural explanation of how to find the answer, leaving the students in the role of recording what the teacher says.
>
> If you raise the level of content *and* the knowledge and skill of teachers without changing the role of the student in the instructional process, you get another version of what we see with some frequency in American classrooms: Teachers are doing all, or most, of the work, exercising considerable flair and control in the classroom, and students are sitting passively watching the teacher perform. (pp. 25–26)

I don't intend for this book to be a manifesto about how to improve American education; rather, it acts as a reminder that we already know what to do. While new ideas and innovative practices, programs, and pedagogies are exciting, this book will make the case that the simplest practices are often the most effective—that common sense, while not as common as it ought to be, deserves our consideration.

As educators and educator leaders, we've overcomplicated the work. In some cases, we have engaged in and continued to pursue practices that have less-than-optimal effects on student learning. In others, we have insufficiently committed to a course of action that has proven to achieve good results. The reasons behind these approaches are many and varied, but each reason fails to take into account the ultimate purpose of education: to foster learning in our students. As a result, this book encourages educators and educator leaders to focus on learning by first turning or returning to teaching practices that have proven results in classrooms—and that are simply common sense.

Each chapter in this book will describe teaching strategies or practices currently used in classrooms that simply don't work. It will then describe common-sense alternative practices that are research based and have proven success in schools where I have worked. Each chapter will feature examples and recommendations for strengthening or introducing these common-sense ideas in your school or schools. These examples and insights come from my experiences as a site principal and district office administrator in excellent, successful, and award-winning schools and school systems. Among them, I include my continuing experiences with Irvine Unified School District in California, one of the best school systems in the United States. Throughout, the chapters will show how the common-sense ideas tie in with the most common-sense practice of all—working as a professional learning community (PLC). Often, the ideas presented will align with one or more of the four critical questions of PLCs: (1) What do we expect our students to learn and be able to do? (2) How will we know they have learned it? (3) How will we respond when they haven't learned it? and (4) How will we respond if they already know it? (DuFour, DuFour, Eaker, Many, & Mattos, 2016). We can only optimize the ideas when we have the collaborative foundation of PLC at Work™ in place. Finally, each chapter will conclude with a series of next steps that will allow educators and educator leaders to analyze their current practices, consider the best practices and strategies suggested in the chapter, and create *stop-doing* and *start-doing plans* to improve the work of their classrooms, schools, and districts. While the ideas shared in the book are not necessarily new, initiating or reinitiating these practices will represent something new. We cannot continue to add initiatives (as represented within the start-doing lists) without also committing to de-emphasizing or discontinuing existing practices; quality will be compromised by quantity.

In the following sections, this introduction will discuss some general common-sense notions educators should be aware of when applying the practices discussed in this book. First, it will discuss the initiative fatigue that plagues many schools, and how schools can overcome this fatigue. Second, it will describe the groundwork that sets up schools for success—PLC at Work—and how this common-sense idea supports educators in their efforts to support students. Third, it will showcase an example from my own teaching career that highlights that, despite initiative fatigue, school and district leaders can and do have the power to effect student change if they set their minds to it. The introduction will conclude by introducing the ten common-sense leadership practices presented in this book's chapters.

The Reality of Initiative Fatigue

The quality of new ideas is more impactful than the quantity of new ideas. In fact, having too many new initiatives is counterproductive and leads to fatigue. It's common sense that thoughtfully considered, prepared, planned, implemented, and monitored initiatives are more likely to positively affect student outcomes when they do not compete with other new programs and when we give them the time and support that they need to succeed.

Douglas Reeves (2011) reports that focus is a key attribute of educational leaders. He finds that schools with more than six initiatives experience less success than schools with a more targeted plan. Additionally, Michael Fullan's (2010) book *Motion Leadership* describes the importance of teacher ownership of and involvement in systemwide change. Fullan (2010) notes that compliance mandates never result in substantive, sustained change, particularly when systems introduce too many disconnected changes in a short period, or leaders fail to describe a vision for the initiatives' interconnectedness.

The exceptional district in which I work—Irvine Unified School District—involves all stakeholders in committees when significant change is necessary. When consensus is reached, the district establishes, communicates, and follows a multiyear plan. To extend and apply Reeves's suggestions, we have committed to creating start-doing, keep-doing, and stop-doing lists whenever we introduce a change, a shift, or a new practice. The individuals closest to implementation—typically teacher teams—should construct these lists with the approval and encouragement of their school and district supervisors. In our district, we attempt to limit fatigue by committing to multiyear goals (as opposed to a new initiative each year) and by constantly connecting new ideas and practices to the principles of PLC at Work. (The Next Steps reproducibles that end each chapter of this book encourage you to make similar lists. Visit **go.SolutionTree.com/leadership** to download the free reproducibles in this book.) Last, all new practices connect to the PLC process and the learning cycle that serves as the foundation for all work.

If we want to improve student learning—in a classroom, within a school, and across a district—clearly the big-picture common-sense idea is to thoughtfully limit the number of initiatives that we introduce.

The Groundwork for Success: PLC at Work

No educator since Benjamin Bloom has had a more transformative impact on education than Richard DuFour. In 1956, Benjamin Bloom developed his taxonomy of learning and the foundational practices of response to intervention (see chapter 2, page 31). Bloom's contributions were transformative, reshaping what rigor should look like in classrooms and demonstrating that learning for all is possible when schools develop and implement systems of supports to meet all students' anticipatable needs. DuFour's contributions have also been transformative, significantly shifting the way schools operate and the way teachers work (DuFour, DuFour, Eaker, & Karhanek, 2004; DuFour, DuFour, Eaker, & Many, 2010; DuFour et al., 2016; DuFour, Eaker, & DuFour, 2005). Whereas other educators since the 1960s have greatly improved the quality of the work we do, DuFour's impact with PLC at Work has redefined the nature of the work itself, in ways that simply make sense.

Prior to this notion, other teachers, including me, accepted the notion that one's classroom was distinct from other classrooms as fact. While we may have attended professional development together and used the same textbook, people did not question the privilege of the teacher's autonomy in the classroom. When I became a principal, the teachers within each grade level had worked in isolation, emphasizing different priorities, teaching in various sequences, assessing in different ways, and even expecting different levels of mastery. Collaboration and collective responsibility just weren't possible because we did things in vastly different ways. The major contributing factor to us quadrupling student achievement at a schoolwide Title I school in four years was our commitment to the PLC at Work process.

Educators have gone from those loosely connected silos of independent contractors to collaborative teams, with their commitment to collaboration and their outcome-driven ethos, being the most widely known and employed set of behaviors guiding educators' work. The three big ideas of a PLC at Work—(1) a collaborative culture and collective responsibility, (2) a focus on learning, and (3) a focus on results—reflect the working norms of 21st century learning organizations (DuFour et al., 2016). As researchers Peter M. Senge, Richard B. Ross, Bryan J. Smith, Charlotte Roberts, and Art Kleiner (1994) note, "We are at a point in time where teams are recognized as a critical component of every enterprise—the predominant unit for decision making and getting things done" (p. 354). Successful organizations simply would never consider, and would never allow, individuals to work in isolation.

Michael Fullan (2000) reports, "The main enemies of large-scale reform are overload and extreme fragmentation" (p. 581). PLC at Work mitigates these risks, at both the team level and the broader system level, by reducing fragmentation. It's common sense: many hands make light work. The way educators work together is more important than the work of individual teachers (Bryk, Sebring, Allensworth, Luppescu, & Easton, 2010; DeAngelis & Presley, 2011). The research-based and practical way in which educators can effect change that supports all students is by enthusiastically, authentically embracing and implementing PLC at Work. My favorite single source is *Learning by Doing* (DuFour et al., 2016).

The Power to Effect Change

Along with the initiative fatigue that plagues modern educators, a notion may arise that initiatives are predominantly ineffectual—and that these strategies exist more to assuage critics than to do something that helps. However, the point of the practices detailed in this book is that they are not newfangled ideas dreamed up on a whim. Rather, they are simple, grounded in research, and *effective* at improving student learning.

Consider the following real-world example, an example of information we have about perhaps the most vital single skill that students will develop in school: literacy. As educators, we know what to do and how successful we can be; we are not yet applying the common-sense and tested principles of ensuring that all students can read well. Consider this: it's commonly known that far too many students do not read at grade level—that far too many students are essentially and functionally illiterate. In fact, two-thirds of U.S. students read below grade level (Rampey, Dion, & Donahue, 2009). While there are many problems in education that we don't know how to solve, "reading failure in elementary school isn't one of them" (Slavin, 2018).

As Richard Allington (2011) reports, studies have shown that virtually every student (98 percent of students, to be exact) could be reading at grade level by the end of first grade (Mathes et al., 2005; Phillips & Smith, 2010; Scanlon, Gelzheiser, Vellutino, Schatschneider, & Sweeney, 2010; Shaywitz, 2003; Vellutino, Scanlon, Zhang, & Schatschneider, 2008). The National Reading Panel's (2000) final report clearly outlines what educators need to do to ensure that all students end the school year reading at grade level. It recommends the following (National Reading Panel, 2000).

- Build phonemic awareness skills.
- Develop phonics skills.
- Practice reading more fluently, with greater speed, accuracy, and expression.
- Guide reading aloud, providing feedback.
- Teach students to make meaning of new vocabulary words, in context and separately.
- Culminate in employing comprehension strategies so that students read not to finish a passage but to make meaning. (Interestingly, the strategy of summarization, a high-leverage strategy, is specifically mentioned.)

In multiple schools in which I have worked—Richard Henry Dana Elementary School in Capistrano Unified School District, Heritage Elementary School in Garden Grove Unified School District, and multiple schools in Chicago Public Schools—we set the goal of students' ending preschool, kindergarten, and every subsequent grade level with the reading skills necessary for success. Setting that goal is simply common sense—every day a student is behind in reading is a day that student is at risk of becoming frustrated, of feeling unsuccessful, of failing to access text, and of struggling to learn in any and all content areas. Additionally, ensuring that every student enters the subsequent grade reading at grade level has a much lower cost than the current system of remediation, special education, and grade retention. It's not a simple task, but the process is clear.

With that goal in mind, the educators at these schools did exactly what they knew would improve student reading skills: they placed a laser-like focus on reading and implemented the National Reading Panel's (2000) recommendations. With this common-sense approach, these schools more than doubled the percentage of students reading at grade level. Significant improvements occurred within a year, and were sustained in the succeeding years. Teachers felt empowered and that they were making a difference. While not all students closed the gap to grade-level proficiency, all students positively and adequately responded to intervention.

While we, as educators, have known what to do for decades in many cases (Vygotsky's work dates to the beginning of the 20th century, Bloom's 1956 work to the middle), we now have greater clarity of what works than we have ever had before. Whether from Marzano (2017; Marzano, Pickering, & Pollock, 2001) or Hattie (2009, 2012), the research on which practices are best is clearer than ever. Readers will find this research depicted in the ten common-sense ideas that this book represents.

The Ten Common-Sense Leadership Practices

Within this book, each chapter will describe a common-sense practice that has proven to transform schools and student learning and to sustain success. For each common-sense practice, I will describe the following.

- Practices that educational professionals have historically done, and are still doing, that defy common sense
- The research and best practices that confirm what we ought to be doing
- Examples, samples, and suggestions we can glean from schools, school leaders, and classroom teachers

Chapter 1: Teaching Less so Students Learn More

Educators have mistakenly been trying to cover huge amounts of content as if it were all equally important, favoring breadth over depth, coverage over mastery, and teaching over learning. This has been the result of many factors, beginning with the standards movement in the 1980s, the impact of state standardized tests that assess everything (although they do not assess the standards equally), and educators and educator leaders doing their best to follow curriculum guides with fidelity. While framework and standards documents are essential guides, and textbooks are helpful resources, teacher teams need to design their own curricular pathways more often than they have. Otherwise, curriculum maps and pacing guides are too rigid or, in some cases, well-intentioned fiction. We know from experts like Grant Wiggins and Jay McTighe (1998), Robert Marzano et al. (2001), Mike Schmoker (2018), and Douglas Reeves (2014) that *teaching more* actually conflicts with *learning more*. This chapter will describe examples of schools that have instead favored depth, rigor, and differentiation and provide evidence that this common-sense approach is better for all learners. It will highlight that educators can best prepare students for success this year, next year, in college or career, in life, or on the high-stakes test when they focus. This focus will also dramatically improve the success of PLC at Work.

Chapter 2: Predicting and Preventing Challenges

We can predict that we will serve students with varied needs; as a result, we must be ready for such situations. The *wait to fail* model that exists for identifying students who need support is educational malpractice. We have effectively but tragically created systems that result in learning for some, rather than learning for all. Labels, tracking, grade retention, delayed supports, and overdiagnoses and misdiagnoses of learning needs have been predictable outcomes. Benjamin Bloom (1956) designed a better system. Whether we call it *response to intervention* (RTI) or *multitiered system of supports* (MTSS)—throughout the book, I will refer to such supports as *RTI*—proactively meeting student needs is common sense.

Chapter 3: Letting Students Do the Talking and the Learning

In 2018, more than half of the secondary classrooms I visited across the United States, both in my own district and others, had students sitting in rows. Too many classrooms look like the classrooms of 1950. Students *sit and get*: for most of the day, the teacher talks, and the students listen. Learning, to the extent that it occurs, is passive. Lev Vygotsky (1978) developed the theories that prove the illogic of passive learning at the beginning of the 20th century. Charlotte Danielson (2008), Robert

Marzano (2009), John Spencer and A. J. Juliani (2017), Trevor MacKenzie (2016), and the National Research Council (2000) have more recently confirmed that the ones doing the thinking, talking, and doing are indeed the ones doing the learning. Inquiry-based approaches, the teacher-as-facilitator role, and rich, frequent, and—at least initially—scaffolded opportunities for students to collaborate and communicate must become the norm in our classrooms.

Chapter 4: Keeping Learning Targets Visible and Still

Teachers must make what they ask students to know, do, and learn clear for students. The content of a homework assignment, quiz, or test should not be a mystery. This does not, of course, mean that tests should be identical to a review sheet; assessments should ask students to demonstrate their understanding in unique contexts. However, students shouldn't feel the need to ask, "What's going to be on the test, Mr. Weber?" It's common sense: students can hit any target they can see. Additionally, the target needs to hold still long enough for them to hit it. One-time chances to demonstrate understanding defy common sense. Some students will need more time to learn or display understanding because not all students learn at the same rate. This does not mean these students can't or won't learn, but they certainly can't and won't if we don't give them the opportunities, and these opportunities can be neither general (like study halls) nor voluntary. Rick Stiggins (2006), Grant Wiggins and Jay McTighe (1998), Larry Lezotte and Kathleen McKee Snyder (2010), Benjamin Bloom (1968, 1974, 1984), Dylan Wiliam (2018), and Richard DuFour, Rebecca DuFour, Robert Eaker, Thomas Many, and Mike Mattos (2016) have done the research and provided guidance for alternative strategies. This chapter suggests learning target trackers, buffer times, and formative feedback to empower students and accelerate student learning.

Chapter 5: Nurturing Behavioral Habits That Affect Motivation

The great majority of students who experience academic difficulties also have behavioral needs that contribute to these challenges. Likewise, students who display behavioral difficulties frequently have already experienced years of academic frustration. We, as educators and educator leaders, are actively, although certainly not intentionally, eroding student motivation. Motivation is a symptom, not a cause, of many behavioral and academic needs. When students do not possess the skills to succeed, and educators do not identify and ameliorate these needs, student self-belief, positive mindsets, and motivation are likely and understandably at risk of fading. Our actions, practices, and words undermine our best intentions at promoting growth mindsets. Labeling students (for example, as *can'ts* and *won'ts*) unfortunately suggests that motivation is not changeable. Additionally, negative consequences do not change behaviors. Camille Farrington et al. (2012), Gregory Walton and Geoffrey Cohen (2007, 2011), Barry Zimmerman (2001), Angela Duckworth (2016), and Carol Dweck (2006) have described the psychological science that we need to follow to truly improve student motivation and subsequent performance. We should blur the lines between tiers of supports for academics and behavioral skills. Recognizing that a sense of belonging and positive staff-student relationships have very real impacts on student outcomes, we must actively work to successfully influence these critical human variables. We must take responsibility for nurturing students' behavioral skills, attributes, and habits.

Chapter 6: Fostering Two-Way Feedback

No learning occurs without feedback, and feedback goes both ways. As educators, we check for understanding, both formally and informally, to gather feedback from students regarding their progress toward mastery. We provide feedback to students so that they, with our guidance and support, know where they are and what they need. It's common sense.

Yet, too often, feedback comes solely in the form of points and percentages. With summative end-of-unit assessments, students are often surprised by what's on the test and by their performance. John Hattie and Helen Timperley's original research (2007), as well as the seminal research of Benjamin Bloom (1968, 1974, 1984) and Paul Black and Dylan Wiliam (2010) and the practical brilliance of Rick Stiggins and Richard DuFour (2009), makes clear the game-changing impact of feedback and formative assessment. The key to the term *formative assessment* is in its root—this assessment in*forms* future learning. It's feedback. We must move well beyond assessment *of* learning to embrace assessment *for* learning and even assessment *as* learning as integral parts of our profession (Stiggins, 2006). In addition to short, targeted, frequent formative check-for-understanding assessments, we can use highlight and dot grading to inform students about where they are and what they need to improve without the need for points. Exam wrappers (brief reflections completed by students after educators return assessments and assignments) and other forms of self-assessment are also transforming feedback into a partnership between adult and student learners. The two-way street of feedback is a fundamental element of PLC at Work.

Chapter 7: Emphasizing Skills Alongside or Above Content

Multiple-choice assessments, and our understandable but misguided efforts to cover as much content as possible, have led schools to prioritize memorizing over thinking, processing, and applying. We teach students to use the formula, or the procedure, or the steps, or the algorithm, or the rule. We provide mnemonics to help students remember, which many can—for the unit test. However, retention, not to mention the ability to apply these understandings, has suffered. The work of David Conley (2014), the Partnership for 21st Century Learning (2019), and the new curricular frameworks in the four major content areas (English language arts, mathematics, science, and history–social studies) emphasize the critical importance of skills alongside content knowledge acquisition. Isn't it just common sense that students and adults succeed not because they *have* knowledge but because they can *use* knowledge? We should foster this by engaging students with more dynamic multidisciplinary and multidimensional experiences. We can use lagging homework and spiral reviews to increase retention. And we can continuously improve the balance of our teaching and learning by including elements of conceptual, procedural, application, relational, and modeling lessons within units of instruction.

Chapter 8: Promoting Rigorous Learning Tasks

To paraphrase Elizabeth City, Richard Elmore, and colleagues (2009), if you want to know what students are learning, don't examine the lesson objective, the teacher's pedagogies and strategies, or even the ways in which students are engaged within the lesson, although those are all important. Rather, examine the task itself; that reflects what students are learning. Too often, we rely on the textbook to provide the task, and too often, the task is a worksheet that students fill in. Too often, teachers assign columns of low-rigor problems, and too often, they sacrifice tasks of depth. It seems like common sense that dynamic teacher practices and dynamic student engagement will be inadequate in the absence of equally dynamic tasks. Elizabeth City, Richard Elmore, Sarah Fiarman, and Lee Teitel (2009), Barbara Blackburn (2014), and Bill Daggett (2016) provide guidance for increasing the rigor and relevance of tasks. A focus on "teach less, learn more" creates the time for tasks within which justifying, explaining, and applying enjoy a major role. Students' learning experiences increasingly become multiday lessons within which rich learning occurs.

Chapter 9: Empowering Parents as Partners in Education

If we want parents to be more involved and more supportive, then we need to lead them and provide specific guidance on what to do and how to do it. Why would we expect parents to know the ways in which they can best support their children without our input? That doesn't make sense. We too often blame parents, or a lack of parental involvement, for underachievement. Too often, assistance with homework is the only way that we expect parents to provide support, and the only support that parents know to provide. Back-to-school nights and open houses cannot be the extent of our interactions with parents. We can do better.

As is so frequently the case, when it comes to increasing parental involvement and support, we are the answer we've been waiting for. Larry Lezotte and Kathleen McKee Snyder (2010), James Comer, Norris Haynes, Edward Joyner, and Michael Ben-Avie (1996), Michael Fullan and Michelle Pinchot (2018), Eric Jensen (2009, 2013), and Anthony Muhammad (2018) have researched, developed, and implemented frameworks for increasing parental involvement. Districts in which I have worked and schools that I've supported have systematically sustained empowered parents as true and impactful partners in student learning. From reframing the role of parent volunteers to facilitating parent learning of the ten educational commandments for parents, educators I've been lucky enough to work with have taken steps that have made the school-parent partnership a powerful lever for change.

Chapter 10: Inspiring and Enabling Staff Engagement

Well-meaning and hardworking school leaders have too often tried to tackle their challenges alone. We've done too much telling and not enough listening, and too much acting as transactional leaders focused on compliance and rule following. At best, this results in short-term wins and competent management. We can do better; we must do better. Leadership researchers such as John Maxwell (2007), Jim Collins (2001), Michael Fullan (2010), Chip and Dan Heath (2010), and Simon Sinek (2009) have shown us the way. Yes, leaders must inspire, persuade, and continuously improve an organization's (in our case, students') performance; mandating isn't the way to achieve our goals, and pushing, or pushing back against, well-meaning and hardworking colleagues isn't leadership. Leaders must be listeners, learners, coaches, and implementers. And they must share leadership; in great schools, there are leaders everywhere.

A key feature of these ten common-sense practices and shifts is that they do not depend on money or additional resources. Armed with this book, any school or district can implement the practices described in the chapters that follow and begin to make a significant difference in student learning and school success. We are the change we've been waiting for—so let's dig in!

1

Teaching Less so Students Learn More

In 2001, Robert Marzano et al. introduced a critically important concept: a guaranteed and viable curriculum. Marzano et al.'s (2001) research states that the presence of a guaranteed and viable curriculum most significantly contributes to students' learning at high levels. When considering the first question of a PLC at Work (What do we expect our students to learn and be able to do?), a guaranteed and viable curriculum would provide an excellent answer. Texts and standards are not curricula and do not address the first question until educators ensure that they can *guarantee* that students will master the standards within their grade level or course's curriculum because they represent a *viable* quantity of content.

The problem, reported Marzano et al. (2001), was that most classrooms, teacher teams, and schools did not have a guaranteed and viable curriculum. They had no guarantees that students leaving the same grade level or course would master the same standards, concepts, and skills, because they lacked collaboration among team members and made ill-fated attempts to cover all the standards in curricular frameworks. Marzano's research on the quantity of content that national and state documents ask teachers to teach and students to learn led him to note:

> If you look at all the national and state documents . . . you'll find approximately 130 across some 14 different subject areas. The knowledge and skills that these documents describe represent about 3,500 benchmarks. To cover all this content, you would have to change schooling from K–12 to K–22. . . . If you cut the standards down by two-thirds,

you've made it possible for teachers to cover the essential knowledge in the time allotted. (Marzano et al., 2001, as quoted in Sherer, 2001, p. 15)

We couldn't possibly *guarantee* that all students would learn the standards because we didn't have a *viable* (doable, possible) quantity of grade-level or course content to cover within the 180 days of instruction.

Education is not about, and has never been about, coverage. At its core, learning is about *depth* of mastery, not *breadth* of content. We must stop sacrificing the quality of learning and unwisely favoring the quantity of topics over true learning. To illustrate the importance of this chapter's common-sense leadership practice, the following sections will detail educational practices that defy common sense, research-based best practices in education, and strategies and insights for improving student learning.

Educational Practices That Defy Common Sense

We, as educators, try to cover it all, moving from lesson to lesson through our textbooks and treating standards documents as checklists. We attempt to jam as much content as we can into the school year—or, more critically, before final tests. My early personal experiences, and the experiences of teams and schools within which I have worked, led me to equating textbooks with curriculum; there was more content in the texts than days in the school year, and not all lessons were aligned to standards or the goals of the grade level or course, yet we attempted to complete every lesson anyway. The standards movements, including the generation of revised standards beginning in 2010 with the Common Core, may have provided improved guidance, but they do not—according to the authors of these documents—represent a curriculum, and attempting to cover all the content within these guides as if they treat this content as equally important leads to rushing through lessons, settling for breadth of coverage instead of depth of mastery, and inevitably leaving some students behind in our misguided attempt to fit it all in.

How has that approach affected students and student learning? According to Bloom (1968, 1974, 1984; see also Guskey, 2010), many students are frustrated, either by failure to understand what teachers teach or by the shallow treatment that teachers give to topics. Too many students are wrongly identified as having learning disabilities when, in fact, they are curriculum casualties with learning difficulties. Too many students are failing, falling behind, and graduating unprepared for college and a skilled career.

While we are improving our craft—differentiating content, processes, products, and environments; using more dynamic strategies; designing more relevant learning experiences; and promoting greater levels of student engagement and empowerment—there is another variable that we must courageously examine. We must examine the sheer quantity of content that we ask teachers to teach and students to learn. Differentiation, dynamic strategies, relevant learning experiences, and student empowerment take time. Moving rapidly from topic to topic in an attempt to cover it all will never allow for this time that students need to learn.

Curriculum maps and pacing guides are well intentioned, but too often, they are well-intentioned fiction. We intend that all students will deeply master the learning standards within maps and guides, but in reality, the quantity of content makes this unrealistic; the task is impossible before we even begin. Both these many maps' and guides' rigidities and the quantity of standards, lessons, and topics within these documents can make them counterproductive. Fortunately, we have another way to teach to the standards while improving student learning—we can follow what the research suggests.

Research-Based Best Practices in Education

Recall from earlier in this chapter (page 15) the guaranteed and viable curriculum coined by Robert Marzano, author of *The Art and Science of Teaching* (2007), *What Works in Schools* (2003), and dozens of other books that represent the authoritative word in education. Marzano calculated that for teachers to ensure that students mastered all these standards, we'd need a K–22 educational system. Marzano's thorough analysis challenges the notion that students will learn more if we teach them more. In my experiences as a teacher, principal, and central office administrator, students actually performed better on the same standardized tests they had taken in the past—tests that assessed every single standard—when we prioritized standards within our curriculum and stopped teaching all standards as if they were equally important. Standards and frameworks are important guides, but they are not curriculum. DuFour (2015), in *In Praise of American Educators*, describes the differences between *intended*, *implemented*, and *learned* curricula. The intended curriculum is what we plan to have students learn; the implemented curriculum is what we have time to teach; and the learned curriculum represents standards, concepts, and skills for which there is evidence of actual mastery. The learned curriculum is what will lead to higher scores on standardized tests. It's the learned curriculum that students will take with them to achieve success in the next unit and the next grade level, and in college, career, and life. As teams engage in collaborative analyses of evidence—as they examine the extent to which all students have learned the curriculum—they should reflect on how their prioritization decisions may have impacted student learning.

Some may believe that the new standards that were adopted in and around 2010, such as the Common Core State Standards (National Governors Association Center for Best Practices [NGA] & Council of Chief State School Officers [CCSSO], 2010a, 2010b), removed the need for determining priorities and represent, in their raw form, a guaranteed and viable curriculum. Not so. Mike Schmoker, author of *Results* (1999) and *Focus* (2018), notes:

> John Maeda [president of the Rhode Island School of Design] wrote [that] the first law of simplicity is "Reduce." We didn't get the memo... So, too, with the Common Core State Standards. The spirit of this initiative (warts and all) is largely welcome and long overdue: an emphasis on a more authentic literacy and real-world mathematics. But the actual lists of standards and practices were never piloted—ever, by anyone. They are still overlong and abounding in indecipherable abstractions. (Schmoker, 2014, p. 22)

We should create curriculum for our students and our districts using frameworks and standards as the basis for the work. But quantity can't compromise quality. W. James Popham, author of *Classroom Assessment: What Teachers Need to Know* (2013) and *Transformative Assessment* (2008), extends "teach less, learn more" to "assess less, learn more":

> Educators can't teach their students all the things we would like students to learn. There are too many things. Nor can we accurately assess students' mastery of all the things we would like those students to learn. But because educators so desperately want students to learn scads of worthwhile things, we often allow ourselves to believe that we can both teach and test to ensure our students are achieving at their highest level. We are fooling ourselves.
>
> Schools exist so that students can learn. We want them to learn not only a flock of cognitive skills and bodies of knowledge, but also to acquire a collection of worthwhile affective dispositions, that is, appropriate attitudes, interests, and values. Clearly, the set of eligible curricular aims that might legitimately be pursued is staggeringly large. Indeed, it is the immenseness of what we'd like our students to absorb that causes most educators to trot unthinkingly down a no-win trail. (Popham, 2018)

Trying to teach all content as if it's equally important defies common sense. It creates a no-win situation. As future chapters will describe, and as Popham (2018) notes, educators' attempts to cover all the academic content represented within textbooks and frameworks have consequences beyond students' learning content poorly. Instead of teaching subjects deeply, these attempts to rush through content prevent students from learning other critically important outcomes, which Popham calls *affective dispositions*: the habits, attitudes, and interests that students bring to school and develop in school.

Douglas Reeves, author of *The Learning Leader* (2006), *Accountability in Action* (2000), and *Making Standards Work* (1996), has consistently advocated for designing focused curricular pathways that favor students learning rather than teachers teaching. He states:

> If we fail to prioritize the standards, then each classroom teacher will make the decisions for what is covered—and what is not. This can lead to curriculum by default rather than by design. . . . While I find much to admire about the Common Core, there remains much work to be done to make the practical implementation of these standards a reality. Establishing power standards in every district would be a good start. (Reeves, 2014)

Power standards are the learning targets that students have prioritized. Teams do not simply commit to teaching students power standards; they ensure that students master the power standards.

Classroom teachers also favor these pathways that Reeves (2014) advocates for. On several occasions, as a prelude to designing our own guaranteed and viable curriculum, we have asked the teachers of *next year's* grade level or course which knowledge and skills from the preceding grade level or course are most critical for success. In none of the cases have they replied, "Everything." For example, my district—Irvine Unified School District—surveyed high school mathematics teachers with this question, and they identified approximately one-third of the preceding course's topics as essential.

The wisdom of identifying topics that are "important to know and do," those that are "worth being familiar with," and topics that represent "enduring understandings" is not new. These principles, which Grant Wiggins and Jay McTighe (1998) developed and published in *Understanding by Design*, have inspired both international, national, and local shifts in the depth and breadth of curriculum. The schools and districts that have implemented such changes have seen impressive results in student achievement.

For example, the Ministry of Education in Singapore, already performing at the very top of the Trends in International Mathematics and Science Study (TIMSS) and the Programme for International Student Assessment (PISA) rankings, implemented a major shift in 2005. It reduced the number of topics per grade level and course, an initiative it called Teach Less, Learn More (Tan, Tan, & Chua, 2008). Its students' performance on these same assessments was higher than ever in the succeeding years.

In a more personal example, in 2005, I assumed the principal role at an elementary school in which less than 20 percent of students scored at grade mastery levels in reading and mathematics, a performance that had not changed in four years. We made a major first-year shift to prioritize approximately one-third of the mathematics content and approximately one-half of the reading content, and to teach that prioritized content deeply. In the spring of that first year, scores on the same test that students had been taking for years doubled. In four years, the scores had nearly quadrupled (Buffum, Mattos, & Weber, 2009).

Likewise, in Garden Grove Unified School District, a large, award-winning, urban school district in which student performance was already notably high, the superintendent directed staff, of which I was a member, to prioritize mathematics outcomes so that depth of learning would increase. We started with elementary mathematics. In the first year, the percentage of students scoring within the lowest performance band nearly disappeared; the percentage of students scoring within the highest performance band increased by 50 percent. It seems that prioritizing is good for all students. When we prioritize a smaller amount of content, we have the time to dig deeper, to apply further, and to engage in tasks of more complexity.

It's actually common sense that the best way to increase test scores is to prioritize the most critical topics within a content area or course. (Although raising test scores ought not to be the goal, it represents a real pressure for many.) If we commit to a curriculum that we can guarantee all students will learn, because it represents a viable quantity of content, students will likely do better on those testing days in the spring. More importantly, of course, they'll be more likely to retain and apply that knowledge, making them more prepared for next year, for college, for career, and for life.

Strategies and Insights for Improving Student Learning

The research is clear; let's now explore how we can actualize these goals. This section will introduce the following strategies that educators can use to make their students' learning shine.

- Choosing priority standards
- Considering students who require scaffolding
- Addressing standardized testing

- Prioritizing standards through PLC at Work
- Embracing continuous improvement

Examples from districts and schools with whom I have worked, and words of wisdom from educators who have implemented these strategies, will be shared throughout this section.

Choosing Priority Standards

To begin, I would encourage leaders and educators to embrace the motto "Teach less, learn more." This motto reflects the fact that the less content we teach, the more students will learn.

In order to teach less and learn more, one must first prioritize the standards within which the school or district is operating. I use the word *prioritize* because I'm not saying that some standards are unimportant, just that standards are not all *equally* important. I'm not saying that educators shouldn't teach all standards, just that they shouldn't teach all standards as if they're equally important. But how does one prioritize? Catherine Holmes (personal communication, February 5, 2019), Irvine Unified School District's executive director of curriculum, instruction, and professional learning, notes:

> We know that there are simply too many standards to cover thoroughly within a single school year. The question isn't whether to prioritize standards—prioritization is occurring right now in every single classroom. The question is, Do we prioritize the standards using an intentional, deliberate, and collaborative process, or do we continue to prioritize standards based on the number of days left in the year, the organization of the textbook, or individual teacher preferences for content?

We have chosen to empower educators, and accept responsibility for making these critical decisions.

Educators who believe every standard is important and who struggle to prioritize should ask colleagues in the next grade or course for guidance. When asked to identify the essential prerequisite knowledge that a student must possess to be successful in their grade level or course, these colleagues typically very clearly know what students should know and be able to do in the preceding grade level or course.

Also, great school districts often prioritize standards by thoughtfully and selectively partnering with outside experts over a number of years so they can seek collaborative guidance on prioritizable standards and continuous improvement efforts. Karajean Hyde, director of the University of California, Irvine's Math Project, has been a thought partner for Irvine Unified School District since the district implemented the Common Core State Standards (NGA & CCSSO, 2010a, 2010b). She notes:

> Covering too much content means a teacher does not have the time to provide students to explore and understand the topic, let alone have enough knowledge to derive procedures from those experiences. Without conceptual knowledge, students cannot problem solve, which is the goal of learning. Without conceptual knowledge, students do not understand the "why" and "where did it come from" and thus their brains will not store the learning in the thinking or declarative memory. Thus, we see teachers teach the same procedures and steps year after year, as students never truly understood them nor connected them to any concrete learning or understanding. In covering too much content, we end up covering less as we have to reteach throughout the year and every year after. This lack of depth is one of the primary factors that has led to the poor international status of U.S. mathematics. We have covered nearly all the content before grade 8 (much of it by grade 4), and then spent the remaining years teaching the same things again, making no gains in student learning, while other countries who focused deeply on concepts flew past the U.S. in the later grades. (K. Hyde, personal communication, January 23, 2019)

To those who don't believe that educators are reliable prioritizers, I would ask, "Then who is?" For those educators who feel the great responsibility of prioritizing well, I note that we shouldn't do it alone; teams from across the grade level, and across multiple schools within a district, should engage in this process. And these teams should articulate vertically to watch for gaps and redundancies. Exceptional teacher teams nest standards, teach in more integrated and connected ways, and apply skills more deeply to a reduced amount of content. Karajean Hyde (personal communication, January 23, 2019) warns:

> If a district does not collaborate to understand and prioritize what is essential, there is no solid foundation upon which to build each year, and teachers are then forced to try to "cover" what was missing. Rather, if districts come to understand the vertical progression of the standards and which topics serve as vital foundations for the rest of mathematics and life, teachers can prioritize time spent on those topics, allowing students to go in depth to develop true understanding of the concepts, leading to procedures and the ability to apply those in real-world problem solving.

Perfection is the enemy of progress; the bigger mistake is not prioritizing, allowing texts to do the prioritizing for you, or risking that individual teachers, understandably and out of necessity, independently prioritize, thereby creating very unequal student experiences and preparations for subsequent grade levels and courses. The learning cycle within PLC at Work will prompt teams to make adjustments when evidence of learning reveals that's necessary.

Considering Students Who Require Scaffolding

Let's pause to address some logical realities.

- Students with gaps in prerequisite skills will require preteaching supports. These take time.

- Students with language needs will require scaffolded supports. These take time.

- All students deserve a balanced set of approaches (concrete, pictorial, and abstract; conceptual, procedural, and application based; and visual, auditory, and kinesthetic) to learn. These take time.

We cannot pretend that all students (including students with special needs, with language needs, and with gaps in prerequisite skills) can master a quantity of content determined by someone disconnected from the school, the team, and the classroom. Assuming that students with and without these needs can master the same quantity of concepts at the same level of quality and in the same amount of time is illogical. And what are the consequences of rushing through the curriculum? Some students get left behind—in fact, they end the year further behind than when they began the year. Instead, it's equitable to ensure that students master a more focused set of prioritized concepts. All students can (and must) learn essential, prioritized skills and concepts at depth.

Addressing Standardized Testing

For those who believe that high-stakes test scores will suffer if we don't teach everything that's on the test, I have good news: in my experience, and in the schools and districts in which I have worked, the worst way to prepare students for a test that assesses everything is to try to teach everything. The reasons for this are many and varied. Some students won't retain knowledge of the procedures they learned on a day in October for the test in May. Some students will not be able to apply their learning to problems that look a bit different from the ones they practiced. Lastly, some students will need more than a single day or lesson to learn a concept, and too often trying to teach everything results in classes rushing through content. We've experienced it again and again, and it applies equally to students with relatively lower and higher levels of readiness. When teachers set time aside for problem solving and critically thinking of concepts, standards, and skills, all students' test scores go up.

Prioritizing Standards Through PLC at Work

I passionately believe that increased attention and commitment to a teach less, learn more philosophy are fundamental to the continuous improvement of public education and central to the work of a PLC at Work. Catherine Holmes (personal communication, February 5, 2019) agrees:

> To me, identifying essential or priority standards is the fundamental building block to all work that occurs within a professional learning community. To have a curriculum that is guaranteed and viable is at the heart of what a PLC is designed to do—it provides a promise to every student that we won't leave learning to chance.
>
> When we collectively prioritize standards, we are creating a guarantee that every student will have access to the same standards and an appropriate level of support if they don't meet those standards. It ensures that every student enters the next grade with a solid foundation of learning and an opportunity to begin on equal footing with classmates. When we don't prioritize the standards, we create gaps in student learning, and what we often find is that those students with the least advantage are the ones that start with the greatest inequities as each year of deficits builds onto the next.
>
> A guaranteed and viable curriculum is at the heart of equity and access for all students as it allows us to lessen the variations that exist from classroom to classroom and ensures that our collective effort is aimed toward the same targets. Clearly identified priority standards are a promise on behalf of all teachers to all students that no one will leave this classroom without mastering what we deem to be the most essential learning for this grade level.

Selecting priorities also helps guide educators' work in two other critical areas. First, the priorities represent the topics on which our collaborative teams will focus. We simply don't have the time to increase our knowledge about how students best learn all the topics within a grade level, content area, or course. So, we focus our collaborative work on the priorities. Second, these priorities represent the topics for which we will provide Tier 2 or buffer supports (for more information on RTI, see chapter 2, page 31). We do not have time to reteach all standards—to provide more time and alternative instructional approaches so that more students master topics at greater depth. Prioritizing outcomes, then, informs core instruction (Tier 1), teamwork, and Tier 2 (reteaching and enrichment).

Embracing Continuous Improvement

My school district—Irvine Unified School District—has authentically and relentlessly embraced continuous improvement as a way to implement "teach less, learn more." The district was already the highest performing district in the county and among the highest in the state when we decided that *very good* simply isn't good enough. And yet, as recently as the 2018–2019 school year, approximately one-third of students were not graduating ready for college or a skilled career. While this performance would be the comparative envy of almost every other school district in the state, it is certainly not satisfactory. We reached the common-sense conclusion that we needed to provide learning experiences with increased levels of rigor, differentiation, balance, personalization, student empowerment, and depth. However, providing experiences with these elements takes more time than simply lecturing students on rules and procedures. How would we find the time?

The answer was, of course, to prioritize. We determined that we would teach all standards, but not as if they were equally important. We would prioritize those concepts and skills that we wanted to guarantee all students would learn by the end of the year and be successful next year, regardless of any challenges that individual students faced.

We applied common sense, and the recommendations of experts like Reeves (1996), Ainsworth (2013), and Marzano (2017), mentioned earlier in the chapter, to prioritize. We convened representative teams of our district's professional classroom teachers from across content areas, grade levels, and schools, which met for full days and afternoons across several months. These teams reflected on their experiences of what was most critical to know by the end of the year, articulating vertically with adjacent grade levels and courses so they ensured a coherent progression of concepts. We then checked these key learnings against standards documents and frameworks, which also, in some cases, provided recommendations on priority versus supporting standards.

In grade levels and content areas that have external statewide assessments, teams examined these assessments' blueprints to validate the selection of priorities. Teams asked common-sense questions: Is mastering a given topic absolutely critical for students' success in the next year? If so, it probably ought to be a priority. Will a given topic also be a focus in the following year? Then it may not need to be a priority. The process that we followed, and continue to utilize, was more important than any single protocol. According to Catherine Holmes (personal communication, February 5, 2019):

> Regardless of the protocol selected, an essential component of the process is both the input of teachers who will be teaching these standards in the classroom and an opportunity to vertically articulate across grade levels. It's through this collaborative articulation of standards that teachers build an understanding of what the grade levels before and after their own value as the core knowledge and skills needed for success. In working with other teachers through this process, we validate the selection of priority standards and provide a clear vision of how they progress and build from one grade level to the next.

When decisions become difficult, and they do, we remind ourselves that if everything is a priority, then nothing is a priority. And we remind ourselves of our commitment to continuous improvement; we regularly reflect on these prioritization decisions, but we will not back away from the need for prioritizing.

We then created documents that represented our commitment to the teach less, learn more philosophy. These one-page documents, called *years at a glance*, or *YAGs*, are public documents, shared with parents and students. Each YAG starts with a *dream statement* that describes what all students will experience and learn in that particular content area or course, in language that is as free of jargon as possible. The YAG also recommends a research-based sequence that starts the year with priorities for the grade level, something new, and something engaging. These important documents are intended for teachers at all grade levels as well as parents and students, so a document free of jargon helps ensure that all stakeholders understand what all students will learn within a grade level or course. The recommended sequence also suggests a number of weeks that teams might dedicate to a unit. The number of weeks represents the unit's relative importance; we should only plan experiences, activities, and lessons that we can do—and do well—during this time frame. If we spend more time than recommended on a given unit, we realize that this means we will have less time to devote to another unit. We do everything we can to start the year with priorities so that teachers and students have the entire year to attain mastery. Last, the YAG identifies the most critical topics, as well as topics that the grade level or course will explore but that are not must-know concepts. Again, we teach all standards; we just don't teach them as if they are equally important.

You might have made note of words like *recommend* and *suggest* in the aforementioned process. Year-at-a-glance documents are a balance of loose and tight guidelines (DuFour et al., 2016). We trust our teachers. They may know of unit or topic sequences other than those written on the YAGs that make sense for their particular classrooms. Thus, the YAG's sequence of units or topics is *loose* or changeable, as are the order of lessons within units, the pedagogies and strategies employed, and the resources used. The priorities that every student needs to master by the end of the year, on the other hand, are *tight*. We expect that collaborative teams in a given school, grade level, course, and department are highly collaborative; we recognize that there will be unique implementations between sites, and we commit to learn from one another's successes.

Early results from this increased focus on priorities have been positive. More students are taking on-level, college-prep classes than before; more students are earning As and Bs, and fewer are earning Fs. And students report that they feel ready for the next school year and that their stress levels are manageable.

Conclusion

Common-sense shifts in the way we do things take courage, and they take leadership. Committing to the decision to prioritize the teaching of learning of standards, concepts, and skills that the professional educators within a school system have been deemed to be critical represents a departure from the way that curriculum has been designed. A researched-based process such as the one described in this chapter, reference to content-area frameworks and assessment blueprints, and clear communication that anticipates and addresses concerns (for example, "We are still teaching all standards, we're just not teaching all standards as if they're equally important") will guide educators in this important work. It's worth doing; it's common sense. The next chapter will focus on designing common-sense supports for these common-sense needs.

Next Steps

Please complete the following next steps as you consider changes that may be appropriate for your school or district so you can help students learn more by teaching less.

1. Examine current practices by considering the following questions.
   - Do teachers report that they have enough time to teach for depth of learning?
   - Do teachers report that they have enough time to differentiate teaching and learning and to build academic vocabulary, background knowledge, and prerequisite skills?
   - Based on students' readiness for the next grade level or course, do you have evidence or feedback from colleagues that teams have designed a guaranteed and viable curriculum?
   - To what extent do teachers find pacing guides or curriculum maps too rigid to allow students time to master essential learnings?
   - Does the comfort of the status quo inhibit a commitment to depth over breadth?

2. Discover research- and evidence-based common-sense practices by doing the following.
   - Consider redesigning courses and the teaching and learning of academic essentials, empowering collaborative teams, and providing them the time and support to continuously improve their curriculum.
   - Before prioritizing standards, create dream statements that describe what students most need to learn based on teacher teams' experiences.
   - Convene horizontal and vertical teacher teams, and have them prioritize essentials and sequence concepts and skills by examining progressions between and within grade levels and courses.
   - Establish external thought partners within the community or within relevant academic fields to validate the standards you prioritize.
   - Ensure that the quantity of content that scopes and sequences represent does not compromise the quality of learning for the priorities.
   - Recommend teaching the most critical concepts and skills early in the year, even when teachers have taught these topics later in the year in the past due to their difficulty.

- Courageously re-examine the quantity (and quality) of tasks that teachers assign to ensure that teachers spend their limited amounts of time well.
- Early on, create initial drafts of assessments that gather evidence of students' learning of priorities. (These assessments can help establish the targets for which teachers and students are striving and can help map out lesson sequences.)
- Vigorously determine which long-taught topics to deprioritize or no longer teach due to new standards, and hold one another accountable to avoiding *curriculum creep*—the risk that popular or long-taught lessons and activities will creep back into the grade level or course.
- Recommit to the definition and implementation of your new curriculum—it's not the framework standards or the textbook, but the guaranteed and viable curriculum that teams develop.
- Leverage the power of PLC at Work to hold one another accountable to the teach less, learn more philosophy.
- Ensure that district and site leadership does not send mixed messages regarding the commitment to quality of learning over quantity of assignments.

3. Identify what you will stop doing, and develop a stop-doing plan.
4. Identify what you will start doing, and develop a start-doing plan.

2

Predicting and Preventing Challenges

Students in all classrooms—whether kindergarten or high school, college prep or honors—have different readiness levels, learning styles, and interests. All students are different and require different approaches to ensure they learn at high levels. Some students will need more time to learn at high levels; not all students will learn on our timetables. This is predictable. It's common sense.

Some students in our schools have significant needs in foundational skills (in the areas of literacy, numeracy, and behavior) that will significantly impact their success in any grade level and any content area. If we can predict these situations—and we can—then we can prevent the negative consequences that are very likely to occur. We can do this by actively anticipating student needs and proactively preparing supports as teachers, as a team, as a school, and as a district.

Some may call this *response to intervention* (RTI; see Burns, Appleton, & Stehouwer, 2005; Burns & Symington, 2002; Elbaum, Vaughn, Hughes, & Moody, 2000; Gersten et al., 2009a, 2009b; Hattie, 2012; Swanson & Sachse-Lee, 2000; VanDerHeyden, Witt, & Gilbertson, 2007), while others may call it a *multitiered system of supports* (MTSS; see Benner, Kutash, Nelson, & Fisher, 2013; Jimerson, Burns, & VanDerHeyden, 2016). In this book, I will call it *RTI*, and it represents common sense in action. To illustrate the importance of this chapter's common-sense leadership practice, the following sections will detail educational practices that defy common sense, research-based best practices in education, and strategies and insights for improving student learning.

Educational Practices That Defy Common Sense

In too many schools, the first opportunity for support comes when a student has fallen so far behind and has experienced so much frustration that staff conclude there must be something wrong with the student—that he or she must have a learning disability. Learning disabilities are very real, and students with disabilities deserve the very best supports. Waiting for failure (or for a 2.0 standard deviation difference between ability and achievement; see Bradley, Danielson, & Hallahan, 2002) to identify needs and provide supports is not, however, a good answer.

Although schools' mission statements might not include the phrase "learning for some," in too many schools, "learning for some" is a reality. A close cousin to "learning for some" is the tyranny of low expectations, as in, "I'm not sure that all students can learn at high levels, but I'll concede that all students can learn something." In either case, students and society demand that we reject the fallacy that some students will and some students won't or can't learn. Bloom (1971) discusses the mistake many educators persistently make regarding the expectation of a normally distributed grading curve:

> The normal curve is not sacred. It describes the outcome of a random process. Since education is a purposeful activity in which we seek to have the students learn what we teach, the achievement distribution should be very different from the normal curve if our instruction is effective. In fact, our educational efforts may be said to be unsuccessful to the extent that student achievement is normally distributed. (p. 49)

As leaders and teachers, we have sufficiently prepared for the needs that we know exist. Either we are heroically failing to prepare for the student needs that we can predict, or we just don't believe in the mission statement that graces so many school marquees and websites—that all can, indeed, learn, and learn well.

Some leaders too often solve the problem of student differences by assigning students with labels, often accompanied by specific tracks. Ability grouping does not work, for any student (Hattie, 2009; Hattie & Yates, 2014). Others attempt to solve the problem with grade retention; however, there simply aren't many scenarios that could logically lead to retaining a student in a grade. If a schoolwide team (with the responsibility of ensuring that the needs of students most vulnerable at the school) identifies a significant need, then it must immediately provide an intensive and targeted support, and if the student does not respond, the team must continuously adjust the support until the student does respond. If the student still does not respond, which should be rare (Allington, 2011), then the team ought to request permission to conduct a formal evaluation so it can determine special education eligibility. That way, the team can provide even more intensive, targeted, and individualized supports. In most cases, retention should not become an option. However, the practice persists in schools.

I encourage all leaders to embrace a fierce, unwavering belief that all students will learn at high levels—we just need to find the time and the right supports to make this happen. Labeling, tracking, course repetition, and grade retention don't really require more work from us; they place the burden (and the blame) on students. Perhaps that is why leaders have so commonly implemented them. However, research has shown that student achievement improves when we initiate other steps.

Research-Based Best Practices in Education

Designing and implementing systems of supports for students is common sense in action. RTI's tiers of supports represent schools' systematic approaches to addressing the common-sense reality that "if it's predictable, it's preventable."

Anticipating that some students will need additional supports is *predictable*. Anticipating that students will become frustrated and fall further behind in the absence of proactively planned supports is *predictable*. An outcome of frustrated students who fall further and further behind is *preventable*.

We need to regularly ask, "What student needs can we anticipate? For what supports can we proactively plan and prepare?" Collaborative teams must continuously ask, "To what extent are students responding to instruction and intervention?" As we ask these questions, we will likely come up with the following three answers (Weber, 2016).

1. We can predict that students will bring different learning styles, interests, and readiness levels to core learning environments. (Let's prevent frustration and wasted time by readying ourselves with differentiated supports, particularly scaffolded supports, so that highly vulnerable students can successfully access priorities.)

2. We can predict that some students will need more time to master core priorities and that other students will benefit from enrichment within and toward the conclusion of units of instruction. We can predict that not all students will learn on our timetables or in response to our first best instruction. (Let's prevent students from falling behind and from missing opportunities to reach greater depths of learning by embedding time for supports into our unit plans.)

3. We can predict that some students coming to us at the beginning of each new school year will have significant deficits in foundational skills. (Let's prevent continued failure and frustration by providing students with immediate, intensive, and targeted supports that explicitly address these needs.)

These three scenarios, which align to the three tiers of RTI, are realities for which we can prepare and situations that should not surprise. RTI does not have three tiers because some wise sage dictated from on high that three tiers were best. It has three tiers because there are three predictable types of supports that we can anticipate students will need. The scenarios describe what we do, and the reason for doing it, at each tier.

Visible Learning reports that RTI has an effect size that places this schoolwide support system in the top five practices in which schools can engage, out of over two hundred such practices (Hattie, 2009; Hattie & Yates, 2014). Historically, the research of Benjamin Bloom (1968, 1974, 1984), dating from the 1960s, validates the efficacy of RTI, and Tom Guskey (2010) has interpreted Bloom's work for the modern educator. Reading experts Richard Allington (2011) and Robert Slavin (2018) both highlight the effectiveness of RTI, and note that we're not doing it as well as we can. My research and practice, with Austin Buffum, Mike Mattos, and Tom Hierck (Buffum, Mattos, Weber, & Hierck, 2015; Buffum, Mattos, & Weber, 2009, 2010, 2011; Weber, 2015), also confirm the transformative impacts of designing and implementing systems of supports that proactively prepare for students' anticipated needs. These systems of supports, whether named RTI or MTSS, are among the most research-based initiatives with which educators can engage (Burns et al., 2005; Burns & Symington, 2002; Elbaum et al., 2000; Gersten et al., 2009a, 2009b; Hattie, 2012; Swanson & Sachse-Lee, 2000; VanDerHeyden et al., 2007).

The following section will detail strategies through which leaders can implement systems of supports to improve student learning. It will also provide helpful advice from leaders in the field to guide leaders on their journeys.

Strategies and Insights for Improving Student Learning

RTI is:

a process for responding to students' needs as soon as the need arises, not waiting until a student falls far enough behind to qualify for special education or until the end of the trimester to intervene. RTI is about prevention, because preventing problems is more effective than treating them after they occur. (M. Wallin, personal communication, January 28, 2019)

RTI is common sense in action—yet I fear some schools and districts, as they often do, overcomplicate RTI. This overcomplication occurs when the documentation and meetings receive more attention than ensuring that all students are responding to instruction and intervention. In RTI, we gather evidence, we collaboratively analyze evidence, and we collectively design supports in response to this evidence to meet student needs. In other words, we check for understanding, whether formally or informally, so that we can intervene—no matter the type of need, no matter the tier of support. A straightforward way of describing all three tiers of supports that we apply in RTI, whether to academic or behavioral skills, is by using the terms *proactive*, *targeted*, and *organized*. The following sections will simplify the three tiers of RTI according to these three words. They will then discuss several examples of schools that have implemented RTI to improve student learning.

Implementing Tier 1

At Tier 1, classroom teachers meet student needs in differentiated ways as they strive to ensure all students master the essentials of the grade level, content area, or course. Marci Russell is Irvine Unified School District's intervention psychologist. She firmly believes that differentiation at Tier 1 is the first line of defense, recommending that educators and educator leaders "start with prevention first, establishing a school's Tier 1 systems and supports, and layering tiers of support for those students who need it, using data to determine which students need more support and what specific skill to target" (M. Russell, personal communication, January 28, 2019). Let's take a look at how leaders can be proactive, targeted, and organized at Tier 1.

- **Proactive:** Leaders can and should know the characteristics and needs of students who are coming into teachers' classrooms at the beginning of the year. Screening data could provide this information, as could structured conversations between last year's teachers and this year's teachers. In most cases, students come to their new classrooms either from a lower grade at the same school or from a feeder school. (In the case of incoming kindergarten students or students new to the school, we can and should have a process for screening these students prior to the beginning of the school year.) We can meet student needs at Tier 1 by proactively preparing differentiated supports and, in the case of students who have not yet mastered prerequisites from prior grade levels, preparing scaffolds so that they can access the core.

- **Targeted:** Leaders should not favor coverage over mastery. If they do so, they will forever compromise efforts to ensure all students master the core's priorities at depth so that they can apply their learning and retain their understandings for the next year and beyond. Instead, we must target core supports for students, prioritizing the key outcomes for each grade level or course and focusing on depth, not breadth. We will teach all standards, but we cannot teach all standards as if they're equally important. (For more information, see chapter 1, page 15.)

- **Organized:** No teacher can intervene to meet all students' needs on his or her own. Leaders must organize staffs into collaborative teams—through PLC at Work—so they learn from and with one another and collaboratively prepare for differentiated core instruction. The logical way that we can ensure this collaborative preparation succeeds is by organizing learning outcomes into common units of study that include common prioritized learning targets. Teams of educators cannot collaboratively prepare otherwise. It's also logical that we have a consistent way of measuring mastery so that the team (and the students) know what the target looks like. We must be organized, designing common assessments in advance to collectively measure mastery of the essentials.

Alexandra Leonard is an intervention psychologist in Irvine Unified School District, leading the district's RTI and MTSS efforts and guiding schools in improving systematic supports for students. She notes that a lack of clarity on the who, what, and when of these supports can lead to frustration on the how, in addition to overcomplications:

> One of my biggest lessons learned over the last few years has been that when we are not clear on our expectations or definitions of [RTI's] elements, it makes it more challenging and difficult for sites to implement and develop the framework to fit their site needs. I also believe that sometimes we overcomplicate MTSS by trying to make it something bigger than it needs to be, when if we were to focus on [RTI's common-sense] elements at both the individual student and schoolwide level, we could have a significant impact on all student learning. I also think that as a district, there are opportunities to further clarify our expectations by developing common language around the critical

elements so that sites hear the common message from all departments. (A. Leonard, personal communication, February 11, 2019)

As leaders, we must heed this advice—simplify our approach to RTI, clarify our expectations, and develop a common language—to implement truly effective interventions at Tier 1.

But what about those students who we know will need greater, more time-intensive help? For them, we must prepare Tier 2 supports.

Implementing Tier 2

At Tier 1, educator leaders support teacher teams in providing differentiated strategies that match students' current readiness levels, interests, styles, and needs. At Tier 2, teacher teams collaboratively analyze ongoing evidence of learning to provide timely, collective supports. Let's consider how leaders can be proactive, targeted, and organized at Tier 2.

- **Proactive:** Recognizing that some students won't learn within our timetables, educator leaders encourage teacher teams to embed buffer times and days while planning the school year. Finding times for these buffer times after we have scoped and sequenced the year is nearly impossible. Instead, leaders should proactively carve out times for Tier 2 intervention and enrichment. All students benefit. Dedicating time for these "no new content" periods will mean that teachers won't be able to cover as much content. But not proactively preparing time for these supports has much more significant consequences.

- **Targeted:** Teacher teams certainly cannot reteach and provide enrichment on all the learning outcomes within Tier 1. Let's not try. Instead, educator leaders should empower teacher teams to target these supports on the most critical and prioritized learning outcomes for which there is evidence of need. And while research does not support ability grouping at Tier 1, we can target Tier 2 supports based on what evidence gathering reveals are students' intervention and enrichment needs. Schools can target these supports if educator leaders create conditions that are organized.

- **Organized:** An individual teacher can provide Tier 2 supports. But logically, we will have more success meeting this anticipatable set of needs if educator leaders organize teams' daily schedules (at the elementary level) or the school's bell schedules (at the secondary level) so that teacher teams for grade levels or courses can share students. This way, they can provide supports based on the similar needs that they have revealed through evidence gathering, such as through common assessments. Organization and coordination are key.

Tier 2 isn't complicated. The key is really just building in more time and alternative supports so that students master the Tier 1 priorities at more depth. For some students, that means intervention; for others, it means enrichment. For students requiring Tier 2 intervention, we reach down from the grade-level expectation to pull them up. And, notably, we're proactive about these predictable challenges.

Implementing Tier 3

Tier 3 need not be complicated either. An intensive support that meets a student's need at Tier 3 is simply a core support that didn't meet a student's needs several grade levels or courses before—Tier 3 supports meet an unmet Tier 1 need from years earlier. At Tier 3, we meet students where they currently are, regardless of grade level, pushing them up toward where they ought to be. Let's take a look at how leaders can be proactive, targeted, and organized at Tier 3.

- **Proactive:** Universal screening directly informs Tiers 1 and 3. Just as educator leaders gather information to proactively inform prepared, differentiated supports at Tier 1, leaders use universal screening to proactively provide intensive supports at Tier 3 at the very beginning of the year, empowering teacher teams to prepare proactive strategies. Schools must not and need not delay in preparing Tier 3 supports, since students rarely teach themselves the foundational skills that represent their significant area of need over the summer. And it's simply not logical that a teacher and teacher team can, alone, meet a student's Tier 1, 2, and 3 needs. Instead, schools must leverage the human resources of the entire building to proactively prepare for Tier 3 supports that teachers can immediately provide. Schools are unlikely to receive more money or staff members; instead, consider repurposing the roles that existing staff assume. If you can find a thirty-minute daily time period when a staff member can be assigned or reassigned to providing targeted, intensive intervention (with the appropriate training and a research-based program, of course), then five to seven students who would otherwise not be receiving Tier 3 support will be on track to closing the gap toward grade-level expectations.

- **Targeted:** The best intervention is a targeted intervention. A broad support in, for example, the area of reading is a very inefficient, and perhaps unnecessary, way of intervening at Tier 3. A better approach would be to listen to a student read, determine the most immediate area of need and the primary cause of the difficulty—either phonological awareness, simple phonics, advanced phonics, fluency, or comprehension—and target an intervention accordingly.

- **Organized:** Few if any schools have enough staff to schedule separate grades 4, 5, and 6 advanced phonics Tier 3 intervention sessions. So educator leaders must ensure that time is organized, scheduling strategically across grades and grade spans. It will likely result in an intervention schedule that works in concert with the core class schedule. For example, subject areas from which students with the most significant needs may be temporarily pulled so that they can receive life-changing reading intervention will need to be aligned across, for example, grades 4–5 or grades 7–8, given that students from multiple grade levels will likely be within a Tier 3 reading group. Few schools have enough staff to provide separate, grade-level-specific interventions, and these groups should be focused on students' current level of needs, not their age or grade level. This is possible, of course, because we provide Tier 3 supports that correspond with students' current readiness level, not their grade level.

At its core, RTI is an organized, passionate commitment to every single student learning at high levels. If leaders apply these principles, research shows that these supports will have a substantial impact on student learning. My personal experiences in schools, as well as considerable research, attest to this fact (Burns et al., 2005; Burns & Symington, 2002; Elbaum et al., 2000; Gersten et al., 2009a, 2009b; Hattie, 2012; Swanson & Sachse-Lee, 2000; VanDerHeyden et al., 2007).

Many schools are applying the common-sense principles of RTI and having sustained success. The following sections detail a few examples of common-sense actions that schools within Irvine Unified School District are taking.

Teaching Less So Students Can Learn More and Get More Support

As noted in chapter 1 (page 15), educators in my district have recommitted our prioritization efforts to determining essential learning outcomes in each grade level, content area, and course so that students can learn more. However, this prioritization also has the following benefits, among others.

- It engages students more actively in their learning (a common-sense strategy described in chapter 3, page 47).
- Teachers have time to reinforce behavioral skills along with academics (a common-sense strategy described in chapter 5, page 73).
- Teachers have time to provide balanced teaching and learning (a common-sense strategy described in chapter 7, page 109).
- Students have time to engage in more rigorous learning experiences (a common-sense strategy described in chapter 8, page 125).

Further, teaching less so that students learn more and more deeply also applies to supporting students' anticipatable needs. Differentiation is challenging; it's nearly impossible if we rush through a text or an inappropriately jam-packed or insufficiently prioritized curriculum. Having committed to carving out the time to meet students' different needs at Tier 1, Irvine Unified School District has acknowledged that we do not know enough and have not done enough to successfully differentiate. So, we have made differentiation a priority across the district, relearning the principles and practices of differentiating content, processes, products, and environments (Tomlinson, 2001); learning more about universal design for learning (Meyer, Rose, & Gordon, 2014); and providing multiple means of representation (ways in which we introduce new concepts and facilitating learning), action (ways in which students interact with new learning), expression (ways in which students demonstrate what they know and are able to do), and engagement (ways in which students are actively engaged with concepts, including shifts to the classroom environment that promote active learning).

Differing educator approaches based on differing student needs, interests, and readiness levels is challenging. Irvine Unified School District starts by acknowledging that the need exists and taking responsibility for implementing differentiation strategies. Our next steps are to build the capacity of all teachers to incorporate these strategies in their daily practice—often teachers learn best from their teacher colleagues who are having successes—and monitoring the effectiveness of the strategies based on evidence of learning so that adjustments can be made.

Providing Supports Immediately

Irvine Unified School District, like many other forward-thinking schools and school systems around the United States, is rethinking schedules, repurposing staff, and reallocating funds so that we can provide proactively anticipated and prepared supports within the school day—ideally, without the student missing core instruction. Additionally, we are intervening immediately and in place of anything but core literacy and mathematics when significant needs exist; such targeted, intensive supports provided immediately will likely be temporary in comparison. Students who are illiterate or innumerate (relative to the expectations of their age and grade) will not be successful now or in the future unless we immediately address the causes of their difficulties and eliminate gaps. This starts with courageous leadership (see chapter 2, page 31).

Implementing Alternative Scheduling

Irvine high schools are making a game-changing, common-sense shift by introducing an eight-period schedule made up of alternating four-period days. With this schedule, a normal load for students is six classes; this allows students time in the day to self-regulate, self-monitor, self-advocate, and generally de-stress. They can also be assigned or sign up for support or enrichment classes, although we are mindful to guide students to avoid adding more and more Advanced Placement or high-stress classes. The normal load for teachers is also six classes out of eight periods, providing additional time for teachers to support themselves and students.

Introducing a Collaborative Class

Our secondary schools are increasingly employing the *collaborative class*, a common-sense strategy that serves students in need of additional supports so they succeed in core, on-level, or college prep courses. These classes are taught by two staff members (either a teacher and an instructional assistant, a credentialed content-area teacher and a special education teacher, or two credentialed content-area teachers, which is our preferred and increasingly used option). Not at all a new concept, these classes proactively provide supports that we can anticipate some students will need to succeed. While a double period of a given subject may accomplish the same goal, collaborative classes provide additional supports in one period.

In our version, these classes are several students smaller than average and are intentionally heterogeneous; students at risk of failure without these types of supports make up about one-third of the class. Certainly, allocating these numbers of staff is expensive, but it is less expensive than having students repeat a grade or a course, offering summer school, or providing special education.

Including Buffer Times

When Benjamin Bloom (1968, 1974, 1984) invented response to intervention in the 1960s (Guskey, 2010), first in large urban Chicago high schools with large class sizes, he started by implementing common-sense supports based on a readily identified and repeatedly occurring situation. This situation is that not all students demonstrate the necessary level of understanding and mastery at the conclusion of a chapter or unit of instruction. And moving on without responding to this reality has predictable (and preventable) consequences: students are not ready for the next unit of instruction, their motivation and mindset wane, and over time, the cumulative effects of not learning what they should have learned look like significant deficits in foundational skills.

So, Bloom built in buffer days between units of instruction. Using evidence of learning they gathered throughout and by the end of the preceding unit, teachers provided intervention (reteaching) or enrichment to students based on their needs during this buffer time. Thus, Tier 2 was born. Famously, implementing this common-sense strategy had astounding results—students made over 1.0 standard deviation of growth in a year, compared with the normal growth of 0.4 standard deviation (Bloom, 1984). In other words, the effect size of Tier 2 is 1.0.

School leaders know what to do; they've known what to do since Bloom's study. They need to include buffer times to ensure they meet students' learning needs at Tier 2. Our schools call these buffer times *WIN (what I need) time* in elementary school, *tutorial times* in middle school, and *office hours* in high school. No matter the name or the exact logistics involved, these buffer times are "no new content" periods during which teachers can address student needs.

Integrating RTI Within the PLC Process

Alexandra Leonard recommends integrating the work of RTI with other high-leverage practices. When describing Irvine Unified School District's ongoing efforts to implement RTI, Leonard states:

> I believe [our district's] next steps include continuing to develop that common language across all departments and embedding that in professional learning opportunities. I also feel that if we could align our professional learning efforts, particularly PLCs, so that we're being targeted in providing support to sites and teachers around each of the critical elements, that would be helpful in not making RTI/MTSS just "one more thing." It's best to start small and to take time to plan before implementing anything related to RTI/MTSS. Identify the critical components of RTI/MTSS, develop a common language and understanding of them, utilize data to evaluate the current state and areas of need, identify existing resources or initiatives that connect to RTI/MTSS, and develop a plan for implementation, starting small, maybe a cohort of schools to build models. (A. Leonard, personal communication, February 11, 2019)

RTI, while a powerful, school-changing, and proven set of principles and practices, will not be successful unless combined with the principles and practices of PLCs.

Conclusion

Preventing learning difficulties by proactively preparing for needs that we have the evidence and ability to predict is common sense, and it's one of the most systematic and effective actions that schools can take. We can predict that students within our core classroom will have differing learning styles, interests, needs, and current readiness levels. Let's be ready with differentiated Tier 1 supports. We can predict that not all students will have demonstrated adequate mastery of essentials at the conclusion of units of instruction. Let's be ready with Tier 2 buffer supports. And we can predict that there are students in our schools with significant needs in foundational skill areas. Let's be ready with timely and intensive Tier 3 supports. To make systems of supports more successful and sustainable, I recommend that educators and educator leaders focus on making supports more proactive, targeted, and organized.

Another common-sense notion—one that will likely reduce the number of students who need supplemental supports of any kind—involves ensuring that students learn in a much more active way than is the norm. The next chapter will address the topic of active learning.

Next Steps

Please complete the following next steps as you consider changes that may be appropriate for your school or district so you can prevent challenges by predicting them.

1. Examine current practices by considering the following questions.
   - To what extent do documentation demands (although important) inhibit the timeliness of supports for students?
   - To what extent do all staff (across the collaborative team, the school, and special education and general education) assume collective responsibility for all students' learning?
   - How clearly do staff understand the purposes of tiers?
   - Are the sets of supports that the three tiers represent (based on the definitions provided in this chapter) present in your school?
   - Do all students have access to the tiers of support that evidence reveals they need?
   - What evidence suggests that all students are positively and adequately responding to instruction and, when required, intervention?
   - To what extent do staff consider RTI something that someone else does or something that is for only some students?

2. Discover research- and evidence-based common-sense practices by doing the following.
   - Consider ways in which you could both better systematize and streamline the processes for initiating Tier 2 and 3 supports (from identifying students, to determining needs and supports, to monitoring effectiveness, to making adjustments).
   - Strive to ensure that documentation demands do not act as a barrier or gatekeeper to students' receiving supports in a timely manner.
   - Revitalize and recommit to universal screening processes. Ensure that you provide differentiated Tier 1 supports and intensive Tier 3 supports to students in need at the very beginning of the school year; base these supports on evidence gathered toward the end of the previous year (or prior to the beginning of the year for incoming students).

- Consider initiating or re-energizing RTI efforts by providing Tier 2 buffer supports. To do this, have teams agree on priorities within an upcoming unit for which they will gather common evidence of learning, to determine which students have and have not yet demonstrated mastery and provide collective supports (intervention and enrichment) during common times. Ideally, no new Tier 1 instruction or Tier 3 supports will occur during these common times.

- Consider focusing Tier 3 academic supports on reading in the beginning; after identifying students in need, determine whether their needs exist in the areas of phonological awareness, multisensory awareness (if an auditory processing need is suspected), simple phonics, advanced phonics, fluency, or comprehension. Then provide and monitor the effectiveness of targeted supports in the domain (or set of skills) of most immediate need.

- Be mindful that you do not discontinue Tier 3 supports prematurely. Students with significant reading, writing, numeracy, or behavioral needs will need time (possibly more than six weeks) to catch up; if students are making adequate progress, continue the supports, even across school years. You may find it appropriate to refer a student for comprehensive assessment so you can determine his or her eligibility for special education services. However, a student may not need the assessment (or not need the referral for assessment yet) if monitoring shows the student has positively responded to the supports and they have placed the student on track to close the gap between current and desired levels of achievement.

3. Identify what you will stop doing, and develop a stop-doing plan.

4. Identify what you will start doing, and develop a start-doing plan.

3
Letting Students Do the Talking and the Learning

Teachers who are subjected to lecture-based professional learning express sentiments that should provide all the common-sense evidence we need regarding this teaching style's ineffectiveness. When educators sit through lecture-based professional learning, they feel bored and disengaged, wishing they had opportunities to interact with their colleagues and to apply new learning to their daily practices. Humans do not learn best, or feel motivated, engaged, or too happy, when someone talks at them for extended periods (Brown, Roediger, & McDaniel, 2014; Clark & Mayer, 2008; Dunlosky, Rawson, Marsh, Nathan, & Willingham, 2013; Freeman et al., 2014; National Research Council, 2000). Yet we persist in doing it to students, in classroom after classroom, year after year.

We know that students learn best not by sitting and listening, but by actively learning (Brown et al., 2014; Clark & Mayer, 2008; Dunlosky et al., 2013; Freeman et al., 2014; National Research Council, 2000). It's a relatively simple idea. Students are much more likely to find relevance in and care about what's happening in the classroom—and remember it tomorrow and for the test—when they are allowed to think about, talk about, and actively participate in the problem, situation, or task.

Irvine Unified School District has committed to ensuring that every professional learning opportunity colleagues have together models the active pedagogies, strategies, and activities that they ought to see in the classroom with students. This common-sense commitment is a start, but the real change should occur in classrooms.

This chapter will discuss why increasing levels of active student learning is a must and how we can more actively engage students in the learning journey. To illustrate the importance of this chapter's common-sense leadership practice, the following sections will detail educational practices that defy common sense, research-based best practices in education, and strategies and insights for improving student learning.

Educational Practices That Defy Common Sense

Classrooms today too often look like the classrooms of 1950. For every classroom in which students take advantage of flexible seating options and teachers guide student groups from multiple locations in the room, there is at least one classroom in which students sit in rows and the teacher lectures from a podium. *Sit and get* remains a much-too-common strategy in schools.

Teachers are still directing the learning; they are too often the only members of the classroom community *doing*—thinking, talking, moving, and solving (and I don't think we can count listening, thinking, taking notes, and copying problems and solutions as *doing*). Teachers are working much harder than they should be, while student engagement, energy, and motivation remain lower than we'd like when teaching takes priority over learning.

I was in a high school mathematics classroom in 2018 in which the teacher had assigned a task and allowed for student interaction. Students were working with one another, making sense of problems and arriving at solutions together. However, students were still sitting in rows. Students went to awkward, even humorous, lengths to collaborate with one another, stretching across the aisles to examine each other's work and suggest next steps. Imagine the improvement to the students' experience and learning had they sat in cooperative groups and received guidance on how to collaborate with one another—on how to take ownership of their learning.

Of course, balance matters. There will still be opportunities when the teacher metacognitively models the thinking and problem solving needed to successfully engage in or complete a task. But this modeling need not always occur at the beginning of the lesson, and it need not occur for the entire lesson. There may still be times when students sit in rows, but seating arrangements and classroom environments that promote collaboration, communication, creativity, and critical thinking must increasingly become the norm.

It might be more efficient to lecture at students, and teachers will certainly get through more content that way, but student learning, engagement, and motivation will suffer. There's another way, a way that makes common sense. People learn more when they're engaged. And they'll become more engaged when they are actively involved in their learning.

Research-Based Best Practices in Education

A key element of active learning is collaborating with peers. Lev Vygotsky (1978) validated this notion many decades ago. Learning is social, and students learn more when they listen to peers, process the information that peers have shared, and rehearse their emerging understandings with peers.

Observational and evaluative frameworks and protocols are gaining in popularity as educators recognize the impact that active engagement has on students' behaviors, motivation, and learning. Several of Charlotte Danielson's (2008) domains within her framework for teaching reference student peer interactions and engaging students in learning. Likewise, Marzano's (2017) instructional framework emphasizes engagement. Bill Daggett's (2016) Rigor/Relevance Framework describes quadrants of learning—the fourth quadrant is where students do the thinking and the work. Increased student engagement significantly improves academic performance (Lee, 2014).

John Spencer and A. J. Juliani (2017), authors of *Empower*, build the case for having students take a more active role in their learning and provide concrete examples of how to do this. Trevor MacKenzie (2016) describes how classrooms can foster inquiry mindsets. Spencer Kagan has provided concrete strategies for engaging students in active, cooperative learning since the 1980s (Kagan & Kagan, 2009). The National Research Council's (2000) comprehensive study *How People Learn: Brain, Mind, Experience, and School* describes how learning, and what people are learning for, have changed; in response to this change, the study encourages teachers to design learner-centered environments and increase students' involvement with one another and with their assigned tasks. David Sousa and Carol Ann Tomlinson (2011, 2018) second this analysis in *Differentiation and the Brain: How Neuroscience Supports the Learner-Friendly Classroom*. Finally, when teachers ensure students are actively involved in their learning, students have the opportunity and the need to regulate their learning. Self-regulation is a skill that contributes to higher levels of learning and a set of skills that students must have the chance to put into action in school, a notion researched by Barry Zimmerman and others (Zimmerman, 2001; Zimmerman, Bandura, & Martinez-Pons, 1992). Students who self-regulate review prior performance, analyze tasks, set goals, initiate work, monitor progress, and adapt.

In summary, research and best practices increasingly emphasize that students learning mathematics should think and act like mathematicians; that students learning art should think and act like artists; that students learning science should think and act like scientists; and that students learning history should think and act like historians. Additionally, collaboration with peers and more dynamic tasks are integral. The point is that students should be more active in the classroom and their learning.

Strategies and Insights for Improving Student Learning

While the traditional sit-and-get method of teaching is ineffective, plenty of historical teaching practices help students more actively engage in lessons and their learning. Jigsaw, four corners, lines of communication, and think-pair-share are all simple active learning strategies that empower students to take charge of their learning. Additionally, the following sections detail newer, less traditional methods that teachers can use to increase active learning in their classrooms. These sections will discuss:

- Creating student-friendly learning environments
- Helping students do the talking
- Finding a balance between direct instruction and inquiry
- Implementing facilitated approaches

Creating Student-Friendly Learning Environments

In Irvine Unified School District, we have made significant shifts in learning environments. Students sitting in rows is now the exception. Social learning, collaborative learning, and cooperative learning just make sense. And, if we want to nurture and give students opportunities to practice the four Cs of 21st century learning (communication, collaboration, creativity, and critical thinking), then students sitting in groups or teams must become the norm (Partnership for 21st Century Learning, 2019). From grade 3 to high school mathematics classrooms, teachers in Irvine Unified School District assign students to groups of (typically) four, and more often than not, each group member has a clearly defined role (for example, facilitator, recorder, task manager, and resource manager). Differentiating learning environments in this manner allows students to communicate and collaborate, and to engage in collective critical thinking and creativity. When students sit and talk with one another, they are more likely to do the thinking and doing.

Helping Students Do the Talking

Active learning requires that teachers increase students' opportunities to do the talking. Douglas Fisher and Nancy Frey (2008) report that in most classrooms, the teacher does the talking more than 80 percent of the time. The one doing the talking is doing the learning, so Irvine Unified School District's goal is for students to do the talking at least 50 percent of the time.

One way to pursue this goal is to assist students with the language of learning. For example, in both elementary and secondary schools in Irvine Unified School District, teachers provide sentence starters and frames for students to use, when needed, to articulate their thinking. Examples may include:

- "My data show that . . . "
- "My hypothesis was right because . . . "
- "The evidence shows that . . . "
- "When looking at the evidence I noticed that . . . "
- "I agree with _____ because . . . "

In a grade 9 science class, I observed one of our amazing teachers masterfully facilitating the learning using sentence frames. At one stage of the lesson, student teams were sharing their findings and questioning the findings of other teams. One team member had the responsibility of sharing, and another had the responsibility of questioning. I observed several students beginning sentences and questions before pausing to glance around at the room's walls, on which posters listed frames and stems under the headings, "Statements that scientists make" and "Questions that scientists ask." After pausing, these students pivoted, starting the statements and questions again.

Student study team strategies (such as numbered heads, pairs check, and jigsaw) also help students do more of the talking—and, consequently, more of the learning. Lisa Schneider is mathematics department chair at Northwood High School. She notes that while sound curricular programs are time savers, the key to active student learning is active educator teaching:

> Student-centered learning is possible in large part because we use tasks that support student interactions between their peers and with their teachers. Just having access to these problems doesn't create the magic; the magic happens because our department is willing to use strategies that are not lecture focused, instead using student study team strategies. These study team strategies get the students doing the thinking, the talking, and the doing, and help hold them accountable for that. (L. Schneider, personal communication, February 7, 2019)

It makes common sense that when teachers facilitate students' collaborative learning, the students will do more of the learning.

Finding a Balance Between Direct Instruction and Inquiry

Ideal active learning strategies seek a balance between teacher instruction and student inquiry. A gradual release of responsibility model of teaching and learning—what many describe as *direct instruction* (Hattie, 2009)—has a place in the classroom, and this model has a robust effect size (Fisher & Frey, 2008; Weber, 2014). When they do this correctly and follow an "I do it, we do it together, you do it together, you do it alone" lesson design, classrooms involve a great deal of active student engagement, participation, and collaboration (Fisher & Frey, 2008). In these situations, direct instruction is balanced with inquiry-based approaches and no longer resembles lecturing. (See Inquiry-Based Approach to Learning on page 53 for more information on inquiry-based approaches.)

During the 2017–2018 school year, I experienced an example of balance when I sat with a group of three students in a high school mathematics lesson at Woodbridge High School. The teacher assigned an open-ended task, and students spent two minutes independently attempting to solve the problem on a piece of paper. Students then had to draw a horizontal line across the paper beneath their independent work. Beneath the line, the groups of four students recorded the results of collaboratively solving the problem for four minutes. The teacher purposefully wandered the room, eavesdropping on group collaboration, listening, learning, checking for understandings, and preparing for the next phase of learning. Bringing the class back together, the teacher elicited ideas, approaches, and questions from spokespeople for each group, confirming, questioning, and challenging ideas. Next, the entire class completed a similar task together, with regular input from groups. Last, the teacher mixed students into new groups and assigned them problems to complete collectively. The teacher had posted these problems around the room.

Students were active. They had to think for themselves, explain their thinking to others, and reconsider their original thoughts. And they worked with two different groups of students during one class period. When asked why she thought her teacher had changed groups midway through the lesson, one student responded, "Our teacher knows we learn differently with different classmates."

Part of finding this instructional balance involves implementing tasks that decrease the teacher's role and increase that of the students. It is imperative to find opportunities to let students do the talking.

Implementing Facilitated Approaches

Achieving a better balance will result in teachers guiding or facilitating learning more often, and spending less time directing the learning, providing the answers, and doing most of the talking and work. There are several inquiry-based approaches to learning. First, this section will provide a description of a general approach to implementing inquiry-based approaches. Next, it will describe argument-driven inquiry (Sampson et al., 2014), in which students follow an eight-stage model to collaboratively explore and complete tasks. Generating questions is as important as, and is a precursor for, developing solutions. Consequently, we will then discuss the question formulation technique (Rothstein & Santana, 2011), in which students are guided through a process of generating, evaluating, and selecting questions that are appropriate and significant to study. Lastly, this section will explore the Five E lesson design, a widely used approach to facilitating or guiding student inquiry and learning.

Inquiry-Based Approach to Learning

Inquiry-based approaches represent a facilitated form of teaching and learning. These approaches contain many of the same elements as more directed lesson designs; however, they certainly order these elements differently, and the purposes and types of tasks and the types of teaching strategies are different.

An inquiry-based approach to learning generally has four phases.

1. During phase 1, students interact with the content or task, either independently ("doing it alone") or with peers ("doing it together"). Either way, they're *doing the doing*. Students may be solving a problem, completing a task, conducting research, or engaging in an exploration. The point is that students initiate the doing prior to explicit teacher direction. Sometimes, the teacher may need to provide a model (or "I do it"). In this phase, the teacher analyzes the thinking and work from phase 1, and the class collaboratively examines and corrects misconceptions.

2. In the next phase, students clarify their thinking through a guided process of summarizing, paraphrasing, and categorizing. This can and often does occur with the teacher; the class is now "doing it together." Within phase 2, the class develops questions or inquiries that drive the rest of the lesson. These questions may relate to misunderstandings that were uncovered in phase 1.

3. Phase 3 is the longest and most important portion of the lesson, when students launch into inquiry—into doing the thinking and doing. It is likely that the class will revisit phase 2 (and even phase 1) as needed.

4. During phase 4, the last phase of the approach, students design or produce solutions that meet the need or goal that framed and launched the inquiry. Phase 4 provides a lesson's culminating evidence that informs future teaching and learning.

Argument-Driven Inquiry

Another facilitated approach to teaching and learning—an approach in which students do more of the thinking, writing, and doing—is argument-driven inquiry. Commonly used in Irvine Unified's secondary science classrooms, argument-driven inquiry typically has eight stages.

1. The teacher presents a real-world scientific phenomenon, and students (or, in some cases, the teacher) identify a question they'd like to examine and a task they may complete to figure out how things work or why things happen.

2. Student teams design their method for collecting data and gathering evidence.

3. Teams make initial claims (or arguments) based on evidence that they gathered in stage 2 and justified through logical reasoning.

4. Teams share their initial claims and receive feedback from other teams, who ask questions about the claims, evidence, and reasoning, before each team revises its initial argument.

5. Teams reflect on their conclusions, making connections to other topics and to broader concepts.

6. Each student reports his or her processes and results, employing the discipline's skills, such as analysis, interpretation, modeling, argumentation, and explanation construction.

7. Teams review their teammates' reports, allowing them opportunities to read, evaluate, and critique an argumentative text and provide feedback to their peers.

8. Each student revises and resubmits his or her report.

Question Formulation Technique

Another facilitated approach is the question formulation technique, a process that guides students to produce, improve, and prioritize their questions. This process has the following steps.

1. Design a question focus.
2. Produce a set of questions related to this focus.
3. Specifically craft both closed-ended and open-ended questions.
4. Prioritize your questions based on their quality and connection to the question focus.
5. Plan for the steps that you will (or would) use to answer your questions.
6. Reflect on the process and the quality of your questions.

Five E Lesson Design

The new science framework and standards, which many states and districts refer to as the Next Generation Science Standards (NGSS Lead States, 2013), do a terrific job of representing learning in which students do more of the thinking, writing, and doing. This framework's approach involves a Five E lesson design, which is not new. Students first *engage* with a concept, typically with a real-world phenomenon that contextualizes and motivates the learning. Next, students *explore* the concept through hands-on or minds-on tasks. Then, students attempt to *explain* their findings and emerging understandings, with the teacher providing guidance, clarifications, and vocabulary if and when necessary; students are the ones trying to make meaning and make sense. The next step requires the class to *elaborate*; students develop a more complete understanding of the concept, assign vocabulary and scientific ideas to their explanations, and apply new knowledge to daily life and fresh contexts. Last, the students and teacher *evaluate* progress toward and mastery of the learning targets related to the lesson's concept; these evaluations or checks for understanding occur during and toward the end of the learning experience and inform future teaching and learning.

Inquiry-based approaches, argument-driven inquiry, the question formulation technique, and the Five E lesson model are means to an end—that end is more active learning. While each approach is represented by a set of steps, we should view the steps themselves as simply guidance; the common-sense ideals that the steps describe are what matter.

Conclusion

It just makes sense—the more actively involved someone is in learning something, the more learning will occur, and the more the learning will stick. Getting clear on what students are learning is also vitally important. Lesson designs that begin with teacher modeling are appropriate; when done well, students will be talking and doing during a significant portion of the learning period (Fisher & Frey, 2008). In my experiences observing hundreds of classrooms across the country since 2008, I have drawn two conclusions. First, teachers are talking and doing much more than students; while these classrooms claim to be implementing direct instructional models, they are not the form of direct instruction described by Douglas Fisher and Nancy Frey (2008) in which student talk is so prioritized. The second conclusion is that students are almost always being told what they should know; facilitated forms of teaching are very rare. To successfully learn and learn deeply, both teachers and students need to be crystal clear on exactly what is being learned and what learning will look like. Clear learning targets will be the focus of the next chapter.

Next Steps

Please complete the following next steps as you consider changes that may be appropriate for your school or district so you can help students, not teachers, do the talking and the doing.

1. Examine current practices by considering the following questions.
   - If you analyzed the percentage of time that teachers talk and students talk, how would the percentages break down?
   - When classes problem solve and construct explanations, to what extent do teachers take the lead, and to what extent do students take the lead?
   - How do classroom environments and seating arrangements constrain or contribute to students' talking and doing with one another?
   - How do districtwide or schoolwide lesson designs constrain or contribute to students' talking and doing with one another?
   - What are the quality and differentiated elements of questions that you pose? Are questions planned in advance? Do questions differ by student? Do questions drive deeper reflection and learning?

2. Discover research- and evidence-based common-sense practices by doing the following.
   - Set goals for the percentage of time that students engage in discourse.
   - Commit to and engage in ongoing professional learning, lesson designs, pedagogies, and strategies that promote more active and authentic student engagement, such as the facilitated approaches described in this chapter.
   - Ensure that classroom spaces result in emotionally safe environments.
   - Arrange or rearrange physical environments so that students can talk and work efficiently and productively.
   - Consider committing to a big, hairy, audacious goal (BHAG; Collins & Porras, 2004) regarding the way in which students process and answer questions, such as the consistent use of think-write-pair-share (students do not raise their hands) followed by the random selection of pairs to respond.
   - Ensure that tasks promote (and do not inhibit) opportunities for students to do the thinking, talking, and doing.

3. Identify what you will stop doing, and develop a stop-doing plan.

4. Identify what you will start doing, and develop a start-doing plan.

4

Keeping Learning Targets Visible and Still

If we limit ourselves purely to assessment of learning, we miss a chance to motivate students, engage them, and involve them in their learning journey and to start with the end in mind. Jan Chappuis and Rick Stiggins (2017), wise assessment sages, said it best: "Students can hit any target they can see and that holds still for them" (p. 42). The point that Chappuis and Stiggins are making is that educators don't need to keep what we ask students to learn a secret; it shouldn't be a secret. It's really common sense: students are more likely to learn when they know what we're asking them to learn and when they know what mastery looks and sounds like. Let's clearly communicate the goals of the learning in which they engage—early and often. Students should be able to *see the target*.

And let's recognize that not all students are the same. Students learn at different rates, and some students will fail to demonstrate mastery the first time that we assess their progress. This, however, does not mean they cannot or will not learn! If we, and students, know that they are not yet where they need to go, and we can predict that this situation will likely occur when students learn new content, then we ought to proactively plan enough time and support for them to learn. The learning target should *hold still long enough* for students to reach it. To illustrate the importance of this chapter's common-sense leadership practice, the following sections will detail educational practices that defy common sense, research-based best practices in education, and strategies and insights for improving student learning.

Educational Practices That Defy Common Sense

We cannot, should not, and need not limit our use of assessment to simply assigning a grade and sorting students—sometimes known as *assessment* of *learning*. Assessment can inform future teaching and learning (assessment *for* learning), and assessment can even be an integral part of teacher and student learning (assessment *as* learning; Stiggins, 2006).

Students should not need to ask, "What's going to be on the test, Mr. Weber?" And students' sincere response to "What are you learning?" shouldn't be "I don't know." Neither teachers nor students should be surprised by how students perform on an end-of-unit test; when targets are clear and students receive specific and timely feedback on target mastery, students will know where they're going and where they are.

We can anticipate that some students will need more time to master targets. Moving on to new units (which contain new targets) without dedicating time to reteaching when evidence reveals the need, and to enrichment for students who have demonstrated mastery, has predictable consequences. Students' mindsets, self-efficacy, and readiness for subsequent units and courses will suffer. Study halls and homework clubs are not solely the answer; even well-intentioned open tutorial periods can be improved. When we make supports untargeted and optional, we allow students a pathway to failure.

Research-Based Best Practices in Education

Jan Chappuis (2005) states that students must be able to answer three questions when defining learning targets' purpose: (1) "Where am I going?" (2) "Where am I now?" and (3) "How can I close the gap?" Paul Black and Dylan Wiliam (2010), authors of one of the earliest studies of formative assessments, "Inside the Black Box," describe the importance of students' thoroughly understanding not just their learning targets but the *point* of their learning targets. They surmise that:

> Pupils can assess themselves only when they have a sufficiently clear picture of the targets that their learning is meant to attain. Surprisingly, and sadly, many pupils do not have such a picture, and they appear to have become accustomed to receiving classroom teaching as an arbitrary sequence of exercises with no overarching rationale. To overcome this pattern of passive reception requires hard and sustained work. When pupils do acquire such as an overview, they become more committed and more effective as learners. (Black & Wiliam, p. 86)

It just makes sense that students and educators need to be clear about what they're learning in order to accurately and meaningfully assess.

Anne Morris, James Hiebert, and Sandy Spitzer (2009) note that creating learning targets and incorporating them into teaching and learning are essential to helping students develop conceptual understandings and connect concepts within and between content areas. They state:

> Unless teachers are clear about what they intend students to learn, it is difficult even to begin examining how instruction might have helped students learn it. More than that, it is difficult to plan instructional activities that would be helpful. So, both planning for instruction and evaluating its effects depend on clear descriptions of learning goals. Being clear about learning goals means unpacking them to identify their constituent parts. (Morris et al., 2009, p. 516)

Learning targets are not simply standards reworded into student-friendly language. Yes, targets ought to be written in ways that students understand, but learning targets should also represent specific outcomes that teachers can measure.

Barry Zimmerman (2001), an expert on motivation and self-regulated learning, has found that engagement and agency depend on the extent to which students understand where the destination lies and where they are on their journey. In addition to explicitly connecting the creation and communication of academic learning targets with goal setting, Robert Marzano (2009) notes that we can and should establish learning targets for behavioral (or noncognitive) skills; the vital importance of these skills will be the topic of the next chapter (page 73).

Dylan Wiliam (2018) says it plainly in *Embedded Formative Assessment*: "It seems obvious that students might find it helpful to know what they are going to be learning, and yet, consistently sharing learning intentions with students is a relatively new phenomenon in most classrooms" (p. 57). He concludes by noting, "It seems obvious that to get anywhere, it helps to be clear about where you're going" (Wiliam, 2018, p. 80). Yes, it does seem obvious. It's common sense.

We need to keep in mind the second part of the chapter title (that students need targets that hold still long enough for them to reach them); it, too, is critical. Bloom (1968, 1974, 1984) reports that the effect size of ensuring that a target holds still long enough (known as Tier 2 of RTI and described by Bloom as *mastery learning*) is 1.0, a terrifically impactful improvement in learning. He finds that giving students more time and supplemental supports to master prioritized concepts and skills increases motivation and time on task; also, going forward, it decreases the time students require to learn content, and the number of students who need these supplemental supports (Bloom, 1974; Guskey, 2010).

Strategies and Insights for Improving Student Learning

In Irvine Unified School District, district and site leaders—administrators and teachers—leverage learning targets to empower students, promote positive mindsets, and inform interventions and enrichments. Heather Phillips (personal communication, January 23, 2019), the district's director of literacy, uses a traveling metaphor to explain the importance of learning targets in a very common-sense way:

> Have you ever gone on a trip without knowing your destination? It can be a fun way to explore a new territory, but it can also lead you down dead-end roads and wrong turns, feeling anxious and lost. Wandering aimlessly can be an adventure, but providing a destination (and a road map) to a traveler who is lost provides a sense of relief.
>
> Students in our classrooms are like travelers exploring a new terrain. Some relish the experience, while others want to know where they are going and might ask more than once, "Are we there yet?" When an outcome is not clearly articulated, it can leave some learners confused and impede them from identifying specific steps in their own learning journeys. These learners are "along for the ride" rather than driving their learning toward the final destination.
>
> When learning outcomes lack clarity, students are relegated to being passengers—unable to navigate because they don't see the connection between instructional activities and assessments and the knowledge and skills they are expected to demonstrate at the end of the course. They are unable to take control of their learning, as they are uncertain about which direction they should head.

Learning targets make the learning journey clear, for both teachers and students.

These sections will discuss:

- Creating successful learning targets
- Providing learning target trackers
- Planning backward
- Incorporating buffer time

Along the way, this section will feature examples from Irvine Unified School District and words of wisdom from teachers, principals, and other leaders who are putting these strategies into action.

Creating Successful Learning Targets

Learning targets, and the success criteria that define what target mastery looks like and sounds like, have always been integral parts of PLC at Work. Collaboratively creating targets and criteria guides all four critical questions of PLC at Work, particularly question 1 (What do we expect our students to learn and be able to do?; DuFour et al., 2016).

To begin, it's important to clarify what a learning target is and isn't. *Learning targets* are rich representations of the rigorous concepts and skills that all students will learn. They define conceptual and procedural understandings and describe students' abilities to justify, explain, analyze, model, and apply. Learning targets do also represent rote, low-level learning, and in this context, they are not the same as daily lesson objectives; a five-week unit may have five learning targets.

But what makes a learning target successful? Heather Phillips believes that learning targets should meet the following criteria.

- Learning targets should be clear. Phillips states, "Students learn more and perform better when learning targets and success criteria are clearly and explicitly communicated. Students need to truly understand what the learning objectives mean and why they are considered essential" (H. Phillips, personal communication, January 23, 2019).

- Learning targets should be written in student-friendly language. Phillips notes:

    Have you ever traveled to a foreign country and struggled to find your way around? If you've found yourself in this situation, it can be frustrating. As problem solvers, we might have someone who is able to translate for us. We might also rely on a book or our electronic device to help us make sense of the language. We need to consider that our standards aren't always written in words that are easily understood by students. Classroom teachers are the translators for our students. If the students aren't able to understand and envision the target, they will have a challenging time producing quality work to meet the goal—the same way a traveler who doesn't know where he's going is bound to wander aimlessly and not end up at the intended destination. (H. Phillips, personal communication, January 23, 2019)

- Learning targets should be aligned with assignments. According to Phillips:

    It is important that assignments in class match the ultimate goal so that students are able to make the connection between the work and the learning target. Knowing the end point makes the journey possible. Sharing exemplars and having the students discuss why these are good examples will help them have a more comprehensive understanding of the intended learning goal. (H. Phillips, personal communication, January 23, 2019)

- Learning targets should be co-constructed by students. Phillips states, "Teachers can work collaboratively with students to design rubrics with specific descriptions based on the work examples discussed in class" (H. Phillips, personal communication, January 23, 2019).

Providing Learning Target Trackers

Teams in Irvine Unified School District share learning targets—a unit's essential outcomes—with students before each new period of learning begins. They present these five to seven targets (within, let's say, a four- to six-week unit) in a tracker, either electronically (with Google Docs or Sheets) or in paper form (see figure 4.1 for an example). Writing targets on the tracker ensures students know what they'll be learning in the unit. Students self-assess their confidence that they have mastered each specific target on the tracker throughout the unit.

They also record their progress toward mastery of each target based on evidence and feedback they receive from teachers. When misunderstandings occur, they reflect on why they occurred, metacognitively analyzing their mistakes. Students seek, and the teacher provides, reteaching support specific to the target in which they need extra assistance. Students commonly ask or email their teachers requests like, "Can I come see you for extra help on learning target 4?" Students and teachers know the target for which teachers must provide a little more time and an alternative way of learning. And, not insignificantly, *progress* is noted on the learning target tracker as learning improves. Teachers provide the feedback that students can use to mark progress, or students can independently self-assess based on their interpretation of their levels of mastery. Or, as you can see in the example in figure 4.1, both types of progress can be noted.

Lindsay Stewart and Amy Aldip, two elementary teachers in Irvine Unified School District, have been using targets and trackers to guide learning since 2015. Stewart states:

> We've been focusing on breaking standards down to their most basic skills and establishing a clear target for each step that builds up to the final standard expectation. For the kids, this means we'll be coming back to it often, and at different levels. They have six chances to be successful and have an "epic win" moment, and they can record their progress toward all six of those steps. If they don't know those first two concepts, there's no way that they're going to be able to conceptually explain the standard. If they do know it, and that's clear on the

Keeping Learning Targets Visible and Still   65

LT Number	Learning Target Description	Attempt 1	Attempt 2	Attempt 3	Overall	Self Master Level	Error Type Attempt 1	Error Type Attempt 2	Error Type Attempt 3
LT 5.1	I can identify linear and non-linear relationships from a table.	4			4	I Got It	No Error	No Error	No Error
LT 5.2	I can identify linear and non-linear relationships from a graph.	1	2	3	3	I Almost Got It	Careless Error	Computational Error	Conceptual Error
LT 5.3	I can identify linear and non-linear relationships from an equation.	2	2	3	3	I Almost Got It	Conceptual Error	Computational Error	Careless Error
LT 5.4	I can identify proportional and non-proportional relationships from a table.	3	4	3	4	I Got It	Computational Error	No Error	
LT 5.5	I can identify proportional and non-proportional relationships from a graph.	1	1	2	2	I Am Starting to Get It	Conceptual Error	Computational Error	Careless Error
LT 5.6	I can identify proportional and non-proportional relationships from an equation.	1	1	1	1	I Do Not Get It	Conceptual Error	Conceptual Error	Conceptual Error
LT 5.7	I can identify linear and non-linear relationships from a scenario.								
LT 5.8	I can identify proportional and non-proportional relationships from a scenario.								
LT 5.9	I can identify continuous or discrete relationships from a scenario.								

I Do Not Get It 16.7%
I Am Starting to Get It 16.7%
I Got It 33.3%
I Almost Got It 33.3%

Careless Error 23.1%
Computational Error 30.8%
Conceptual Error 46.2%

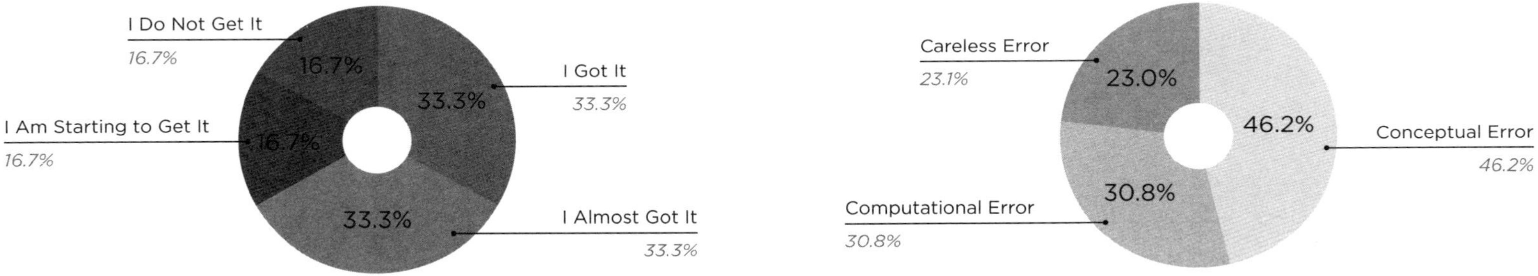

Figure 4.1: Sample learning target tracker.

preassessment, we can breeze past it. If a few kids need to be pulled to go over that skill and the rest don't, that's an easy minilesson. This makes it easier to spot holes, and fill in where necessary.

Students take ownership over their learning and are extremely honest about their areas for growth when they can name what they are. The clearer the target ("kid friendly" language), the easier it is for them to self-assess and say "Yes, I can name decimal fractions in standard form to any place," or "I don't know how to do that yet"). (L. Stewart, personal communication, February 12, 2019)

In addition to providing students with the language they need to articulate their progress or areas of need, trackers also help students understand their own learning. According to Lindsay Stewart (personal communication, February 12, 2019):

The first group of kids that Amy and I implemented trackers with were blown away by how simple math actually is. Their exact words were, "Now I know what I don't know." It was like we pulled back some secret curtain that gave them the words to finish the "I don't get it" question. The targets literally demystify learning, and they give everybody the epic wins and encouragement they need to get better, no matter where they start out.

With learning trackers, the students *see* their progress. It's growth mindset in action (Dweck, 2006).

Planning Backward

Why is teaching to the test forbidden? It's not just students who can hit any target that they can see and that holds still long enough for them; the same applies for teachers. A teacher can and should create a well-crafted, rigorous assessment before a unit of instruction begins; this test, or evidence-gathering opportunity, represents the target the teacher is preparing students to hit and the set of targets from which the teacher is backward planning. Teachers must match the rigor and format of daily instruction to the expectations that are represented on assessments, and the rigor and format of assessments must match the expectations that the learning standards set. This is achieved by planning backward. Lindsay Stewart (personal communication, February 12, 2019) notes that:

Making assessments has genuinely been the most important and helpful part of the whole target process. Having targets, and then talking with your team about what success looks like for each one, is *the* most important part of the process.

We can ensure success for all students only if teachers know the targets.

Let's trust teachers. Educators will not "cheat" by explicitly preparing students for the specific items on a test (assuming we do not attach overbearingly high stakes to these assessments or use results in any way related to teacher or administrator evaluation). But teachers (and students) must know the destination—the success criteria. It's common sense. Teachers should use a unit's learning targets as their guide in designing items and assessments. Educators and educator leaders can more efficiently create assessments and much more accurately measure what we want students to learn when we first determine and define the targets.

Incorporating Buffer Time

As noted in chapter 3 (page 47), if it's predictable, it's preventable. We can predict that some students will not yet have learned the essentials toward the conclusion of a unit of study. We can predict the consequences of moving on to the next unit without responding to this reality. So, Irvine Unified School District follows Benjamin Bloom's advice (1968, 1974, 1984), building in buffer time within or between units so the district's schools can provide intervention or enrichment based on evidence of learning gathered throughout a unit. It's just common sense.

In Irvine Unified School District, we call these buffers *WIN (what I need) time* in elementary schools, *tutorial times* in middle schools, and *office hours* in high schools. They are also known as Tier 2 of RTI. Increasingly in these buffer times, we focus the support provided in a specific teacher's classroom, and during a specific time period, on a specific learning target for which students have evidence of need. And increasingly, teachers in our schools are finding ways to require that students participate in these supports. Teachers do this by building relationships with students (as discussed in the next chapter, page 73), by ensuring that students receive timely and specific feedback on what they do and do not yet know (through the trackers), and through the mindsets that they model and promote.

We have seen several benefits of creating and communicating clear targets with students and using information from trackers to inform supports within buffer times. These benefits include improvements on the following.

- **Mindsets:** Students record their continuous improvements on trackers as their efforts lead to greater levels of mastery, with progress through a unit reinforcing that learning can and will increase with effort.

- **Agency:** Teachers empower students to exercise ownership over their learning; the act of learning and what students are learning seem to have more meaning.

- **Engagement and motivation:** Students have hope that they will get chances to improve, and expectations that they will improve.
- **Assessment:** Teacher teams are designing more accurate evidence-gathering tools, and students view assessments as opportunities to show what they know and see where they are, not only as situations that generate points and percentages.
- **Grading:** Teacher teams are reimagining their gradebooks; they report current achievement levels as mastery of specific learning targets, instead of as a percentage of points earned on disparate activities.

As we have implemented these strategies to create better learning targets, communicated them more clearly, aligned our teaching and assessment, and provided tools for students to visualize their progress, both the learning process and student outcomes have improved.

Conclusion

Teaching and learning are complex. If we aren't clear with one another and with students about the goals or targets of teaching and learning, we make things more complicated than they need to be. And while collaboratively crafting targets takes time, it can help make learning more efficient. According to Lindsay Stewart (personal communication, February 12, 2019):

> So many people start stressing about targets and "fitting them in" to whatever they're already doing. For me, targets have been like permission to skip whatever doesn't fit. Cutting lessons and parts of programs that don't align makes way more time to focus on what matters, and where *your* class needs help. Administering a preassessment may seem like more work up front, but it also gives you "permission" to skip over or spend way less time on lessons that are already mastered by most of the class.

Creating, using, and sharing learning targets and tracking student progress toward mastery of them will likely take time in the beginning, but we will recover that time in the end.

If we don't embed time to give target-informed supports when we have timely, accurate, target-specific evidence that students have not yet learned, we're very likely creating challenges for students and staff in the very near future. Let's apply common sense, like the preceding ideas, to our practice and collectively help improve outcomes and successes for students.

As noted earlier in the chapter, learning targets can and should be rich, defining rigorous, conceptual understanding and applications as well as more procedural, skill-based outcomes. Targets do not nearly often enough, if ever, define the behavioral skills that we want students to develop, yet behavioral skills are as critical to student success as academic skills. Addressing this common-sense notion is the topic of the next chapter.

Next Steps

Please complete the following next steps as you consider changes that may be appropriate for your school or district so you can make learning targets more visible and help students learn more.

1. Examine current practices by considering the following questions.
   - What processes have collaborative teams used, within and between schools, to identify the learning targets represented in prioritized standards and determine the criteria that represent success on these targets?
   - When and to what extent do students know and understand the targets that teachers ask them to meet?
   - To what extent are students involved in assessing their own work, reflecting upon successes and any remaining misunderstandings?
   - What types of responsibilities do students have in terms of knowing the concepts and skills about which they are learning?
   - What opportunities do students have to self-assess where they are in their learning journey, why they are where they are, and what they can do about it?
   - How are students required, and given the time, to strengthen and deepen their mastery of learning targets?

2. Discover research- and evidence-based common-sense practices by doing the following.
   - Consider extending your work from chapter 1 (page 15); having recommitted to prioritizing learning outcomes and crafting a guaranteed and viable curriculum, collectively identify the learning targets—blends of concepts and skills—that students will need to master to ensure they have learned the prioritized outcomes within a unit. At the elementary level, consider starting with one subject area. At the secondary level, consider starting with a unit.
   - Provide opportunities for students, individually or in groups, to make sense of learning targets and demonstrate that they authentically and accurately understand what they are learning.
   - Frequently revisit learning targets and encourage and require students to continuously measure progress toward them.
   - Make connections between learning targets, and from learning targets to broader big ideas.

- Consider getting started with learning target trackers by creating paper-based trackers and sharing these with students prior to new units. Ask students to self-assess their perceived level of mastery of each target on a daily basis.
- Consider exploring technology-based options (such as Google's G Suite) for making trackers more efficient.
- Dedicate regular class time to having students reflect on learning and complete trackers.
- Align short-cycle quizzes and checks for understanding to these targets.
- Empower students to self-assess, self-diagnose, and develop a plan for learning what they have not yet learned.
- Provide the supports and opportunities that students need in order to relearn and show that they have increased their mastery levels.

3. Identify what you will stop doing, and develop a stop-doing plan.

4. Identify what you will start doing, and develop a start-doing plan.

5

Nurturing Behavioral Habits That Affect Motivation

Educators know the importance of study skills, soft skills (such as time management, organization, and perseverance), and the hidden curriculum (how teachers expect tasks to be completed; what is valued, including on assessments, by individual teachers). When students know how to behave—to cooperate, self-advocate, take notes, stay organized, and persevere—they are almost always successful. When students do not possess these skills, they may appear unmotivated. It's not productive for us to lament that lack of motivation causes student difficulty. In fact, the research (Farrington et al., 2012) makes it very clear that a lack of motivation is a symptom of needs or deficits in several sets of behaviors, not the cause.

If we are, in fact, committed to all students learning at high levels, we must address all the needs that students have and all the reasons that they are not yet learning, including behavioral skills. Or else we'll need to rewrite our mission statements. Either we can modify our mission statements to say, "Students will learn at high levels if they care or appear to care," or we can change our behaviors (actions, processes, procedures, and systems) to effect the changes in student behaviors that we believe are needed.

It's common sense: some students will not experience successes in our schools if they have behavioral skill needs. The research and best practices to guide the modeling, teaching, and nurturing of these skills exist; they show us that we are the answer we've been waiting for. (For further information on this topic, see *Behavior: The Forgotten Curriculum* [Weber, 2018].) To illustrate the importance of this chapter's common-sense leadership practice, the following sections will detail educational practices that defy common sense, research-based best practices in education, and strategies and insights for improving student learning.

Educational Practices That Defy Common Sense

Punishments do not change behavior, yet many teachers rely on negative consequences to do so (Sugai, 2001; Sugai & Horner, 2002). In many cases, it's understandable—teachers don't know what else to do. Sending students to the office may have short-term benefits, but the practice defies common sense. Students misbehave for a reason. Behaviors have a purpose, a function. And the purpose of many misbehaviors in class is to *avoid the class*. Sending students from the room will not reduce misbehaviors; it may, in fact, reinforce the very misbehaviors that teachers are attempting to change. Additionally, students are not learning if they are not in the classroom.

We have for too long defined students experiencing difficulties as *can'ts* and *won'ts*. I myself did this in the past. However, labeling students as *won'ts* suggests, unfortunately and inaccurately, that a student simply doesn't care when, in truth, a *won't* student lacks skills necessary to be successful—behavioral skills—just as a *can't* student lacks proficiencies in academic skill areas.

We have also, unintentionally I'm sure, prevented students from practicing a growth mindset (Dweck, 2006). When we do not require students to complete or redo tasks that they leave incomplete or they complete at inadequate levels of mastery, we are communicating to them, whether we intend to or not, that their first attempt is their only attempt and that, essentially, their ability on this task or topic is fixed. Zeros do not teach responsibility, and they do not convince students to start doing work, particularly when needs in academic or behavioral skills contributed to noncompletion in the first place.

I have heard of teachers—excellent teachers—who hesitate to recommend students for college preparatory grade 9 coursework due to a lack of readiness. When we do not provide scaffolds, due to either academic or behavioral skill needs, and instead track students into separate and unequal pathways, we erode hope and motivation.

We lament that students do not seem to care about or find relevance in their learning, yet we do not provide sufficient opportunities for students to construct their own learning, make choices in their journey, or exercise agency. When we do not let students take responsibility for learning, we compromise hope and motivation.

When we do not ensure that every student is connected to someone and something at school, the unfortunate possibility exists that some students might not feel as though they belong. A feeling of belonging is essential for students, as it correlates to both more positive mindsets and superior student outcomes (Farrington et al., 2012; Walton & Cohen, 2007, 2011).

Like it or not, when we fail to make supplemental supports mandatory, so that students reach mastery of essential Tier 1 topics and concepts, we communicate that our mindsets and their levels of learning are fixed. We also communicate this when we neglect to demonstrate *how* (through a lot of hard work) to participate in these additional opportunities, and when we do not celebrate when students make progress toward mastery.

As educators, we do not intentionally compromise mindsets, hopes, motivation, and positive learning cultures, but we have not yet intentionally and systematically nurtured the habits, skills, and attributes that will promote positive mindsets, social skills, perseverance, learning strategies, and academic behaviors. We must do so, and now more than ever, we have a clear, research-based pathway to guide this critical work.

Research-Based Best Practices in Education

From Carol S. Dweck (2006) to Angela Duckworth (2016), from Camille Farrington and colleagues (2012) to Barry Zimmerman (2001), and from Lawrence Lezotte and Kathleen McKee Snyder (2010) to John Hattie (2009, 2012), the research is clear: behavioral skills matter as much as or more than academic skills for student success—and they can be taught. They can improve. More than ever, they can be clearly defined.

The work of Camille Farrington, senior research associate at the University of Chicago's Consortium on School Research, and her colleagues (2012) provides as much clarity in the area of behavioral skills as the National Reading Panel (2000) provides for teaching reading and as the National Mathematics Advisory Panel (2008) provides for teaching mathematics. While Farrington and her fellow experts describe these areas of expertise as *noncognitive factors*, I prefer to think of them as *behavioral skills* because these habits and attributes, like other behaviors, apply in all grade levels and content areas (Farrington et al., 2012). And like academic skills, they can be taught, and they can improve; as Farrington and others describe, these factors or skills are malleable (Duckworth & Carlson, 2013; Dweck, Walton, & Cohen, 2014; Farrington et al., 2012; Martens & Meller, 1990; Tough, 2012, 2016).

Farrington et al.'s (2012) research-based framework describes five interrelated categories of behaviors—(1) mindsets, (2) social skills, (3) perseverance, (4) learning strategies, and (5) academic behaviors (see figure 5.1, page 76)—all of which

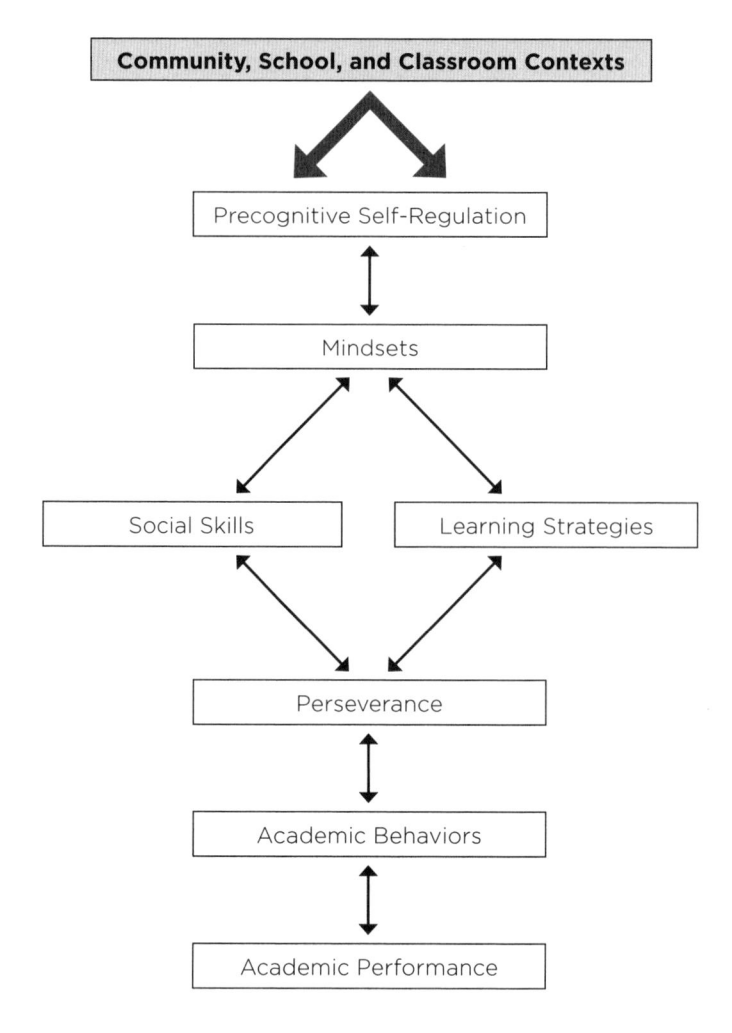

```
          ┌─────────────────────────────────────────┐
          │ Community, School, and Classroom Contexts│
          └─────────────────────────────────────────┘
                              ↙ ↘
                  ┌──────────────────────────┐
                  │ Precognitive Self-Regulation │
                  └──────────────────────────┘
                              ↕
                  ┌──────────────────────────┐
                  │         Mindsets         │
                  └──────────────────────────┘
                         ↙        ↘
              ┌─────────────┐  ┌───────────────────┐
              │ Social Skills│  │ Learning Strategies│
              └─────────────┘  └───────────────────┘
                         ↘        ↙
                  ┌──────────────────────────┐
                  │      Perseverance        │
                  └──────────────────────────┘
                              ↕
                  ┌──────────────────────────┐
                  │    Academic Behaviors    │
                  └──────────────────────────┘
                              ↕
                  ┌──────────────────────────┐
                  │   Academic Performance   │
                  └──────────────────────────┘
```

Source: Adapted from Farrington et al., 2012.

Figure 5.1: Interrelated categories of behavior.

influence academic performance. Positive mindsets foundationally impact positive social skills and perseverance, which foundationally inform learning strategies, which foundationally impact positive academic behaviors and performance. Influences can travel in the opposite direction. For example, difficulties with employing learning strategies can negatively impact a student's mindset.

We can define the five categories as follows.

1. **Mindsets:** Students feel a sense of belonging, belief, and engagement. Affirmative responses to the following statements represent the positive mindsets students must develop and possess to succeed.

- **"I belong in this academic community."** Educators know that students have a connection to someone and something within the school environment.
- **"My ability and competence grow with my effort."** Educators observe that students believe that they can improve their learning with effort—that smart is something you become, not something you are.
- **"I can succeed at this."** Educators know that success breeds success and that a foundational premise of education is meeting students where they are and nudging them toward greater levels of proficiency; students draw on a sense of self-efficacy to persist in learning.
- **"This work has value for me."** Educators know that motivation depends on the relevance that students find in classrooms; students have opportunities to explore passions, they see the purpose in learning, and they experience personalized supports and opportunities for personalized paths.

2. **Social skills:** Students have respectful interactions with others and demonstrate self-respect. Educators observe students cooperating and collaborating in socially appropriate ways and behaving with empathy for others in both academic and social circumstances.

3. **Learning strategies:** Students can regulate, monitor, and reflect on their learning. Educators see students employing effective study and organizational skills, behaving metacognitively, tracking their own progress, and responding appropriately when faced with a task, whether the task is completing an in-class assignment, completing a long-term project, or preparing for a test. Learning strategies can be thought of as *cognitive self-regulation*: students regulate their learning level frequently and make necessary adjustments.

4. **Perseverance:** Students maintain effort and adapt to setbacks; they exercise self-discipline and self-control; they delay gratification; and they advocate for their needs. Educators observe that students stick with tasks, typically because they are drawing on positive mindsets, social skills, and learning strategies.

5. **Academic behaviors:** Students are physically, emotionally, and cognitively present and attentive within their learning and their

learning environments. Educators note that students consistently complete tasks of high quality; that they actively participate in learning; and that they appear motivated to learn, succeed, and grow. Again, educators' observations of academic behaviors typically draw on, and depend on, positive mindsets, social skills, learning strategies, and perseverance, the companion behavioral skills in figure 5.1 (page 76).

Defining behavioral skills according to Farrington et al.'s (2012) model is helpful because the framework then becomes an action plan. We can operationalize the research, putting the experts' best thinking into action to actively support students in developing skills and proactively support students when difficulties exist. Let's say a student is labeled as unmotivated—he or she doesn't seem to care about school, or his or her grades, or his or her future. This is perhaps the most common concern that educators identify, particularly as students get older. A lack of motivation would appear as a deficit in the framework's *academic behaviors* category.

Before considering the skills from mindsets to academic behaviors, we can agree that some students experience daily lives in which home, health, and hunger are very real concerns. A student with an unsettled, even traumatic home life, or one who is hungry or tired, may appear unmotivated and, more immediately, may not display a growth mindset. A student without a growth mindset may appear unmotivated and, more immediately, may not display positive social skills. A lack of social skills makes cooperating and collaborating with adults and students a challenge. Additionally, a student without a growth mindset may not see the point or the payoff in persevering. A student who does not persevere may appear unmotivated, and may not employ learning strategies. Finally, a student who does not employ learning strategies will not likely participate in class, complete assignments, or study for tests, and the student will, in all likelihood, appear unmotivated.

There are reasons—explanations, causes, antecedents—for a student's lack of motivation. When we, as educators, consider behavioral skills within the context of Farrington et al.'s (2012) framework, we can identify these reasons and do something about them. We can *teach* motivation. According to Carol Dweck, Gregory Walton, and Geoffrey Cohen (2014):

> When non-cognitive factors are in place, students will look (and will be) motivated. In fact, these non-cognitive factors constitute the greater part of what psychological researchers call "motivation," and fostering these mindsets and self-regulation strategies is what psychological researchers typically mean by "motivating" students. (p. 2)

What do Dweck, Walton, and Cohen mean by this? Let's do a close read. They first say that when a student displays positive behavioral skills or noncognitive factors (mindsets, social skills, perseverance, learning strategies, and academic behaviors), most observers would agree that the student is motivated. They go on to say these skills or factors are the same as motivation. They conclude by stating that fostering (or teaching) these skills or factors is what the experts mean by *motivating students*. This aligns perfectly with an action plan based on Farrington et al.'s (2012) framework.

Behavioral skills matter a lot to students' long-term life success. Robert Mischel's (2014) famous marshmallow study, in which students' success at delayed gratification predicted future life successes, shows that children with strong self-regulation skills have greater academic and life success than their less strong-willed peers. Research further suggests that executive functioning and self-regulation are better predictors of school success than intelligence tests (Duckworth & Carlson, 2013). Education economist David Deming (2015) believes that both mastery of relevant skills and knowledge *and* empathy are the critical combination for jobs that provide an adequate living wage. Notably, Dweck et al. (2014) state, "Psychological factors—often called *motivational* or *non-cognitive* factors—can matter even more than cognitive factors for students' academic performance" (p. 2).

Further, these noncognitive factors or behavioral skills matter greatly on their own. Chris Krebs (personal communication, February 14, 2019), a visionary high school principal in Irvine Unified School District, has gathered evidence from his decade as a high school administrator that validates the research of educational psychologists, concluding that:

> All students, regardless of their career goals, can fulfill their civic responsibilities and role as a citizen. All students can use reasoning to make informed decisions on public policy related to the environment, health, governance, and equity. All students can show empathy and integrity, persevere, and develop the character attributes that add value to their community. Although not all students can make enough money to do better than the community that raised them, all students can make their community better through their involvement. Through this lens, public schools can be successful for everyone, and show value to every graduate we produce.

Behavioral skills do not simply positively contribute to students' academic performance; they positively contribute to students' civic performance.

As schools and as educators, we simply have not yet sufficiently focused on developing behavioral skills (Boynton & Boynton, 2005; Mullet, 2014; Sprick, Borgmeier,

& Nolet, 2002; Sugai, 2001; Sugai & Horner, 2002; Walton & Cohen, 2011; Zimmerman et al., 1992). We teach academic skills, but we have not prioritized the development of behavioral, or noncognitive, skills to the same extent.

Strategies and Insights for Improving Student Learning

The research is in: motivation can be taught. Or more precisely, the skills that contribute to students' appearing and acting motivated can be taught. Importantly, they *must* be taught. This section will describe the following key strategies to help teach behavioral skills.

- Implementing the six steps to developing students' behavioral skills
- Following the empowerment mindset equation
- Believing educators can motivate students

Along the way, this section will feature examples from Irvine Unified School District and words of wisdom from teachers, principals, and other leaders who are putting these strategies into action.

Implementing the Six Steps to Developing Students' Behavioral Skills

Irvine Unified School District's schools are organizing supports for modeling, teaching, and nurturing behavioral skills in the same way that we successfully organize supports for modeling, teaching, and nurturing academic skills. We follow these six steps.

1. Identify the most critical behavioral skills.
2. Define and make sense of these skills.
3. Model, teach, and nurture these skills.
4. Measure student success in displaying these skills.
5. Provide differentiated supports that respect students' readiness.
6. Intervene appropriately when evidence reveals the need.

We should take these same six essential steps both when developing students' behavioral skills and when striving to help students develop academic skills. Aligning our efforts and initiatives related to academics and behaviors will likely decrease anxieties and increase schools' efficiencies and efficacies as educators complete the important tasks of nurturing both academic and behavioral skills. The following sections will describe what these steps look like in action.

Identify the Most Critical Behavioral Skills

Let's think about the academic skill example of teaching a student to read. Can we teach students to read? Of course we can. Yet I submit that we never actually teach *reading*. We help students develop alphabetic principles and concepts and print. We teach the sixteen or so skills within the domain of phonological awareness (including recognizing and imitating rhyme and alliteration, and blending, segmenting, and substituting phonemes). We teach the skills within simple and advanced phonics (from letter sounds to syllabication). We teach the skills of reading fluently and expressively (chunking, scooping, and phrasing) and vocabulary acquisition skills. And we teach students to apply the many, many skills and strategies associated with comprehension. (Note this list of what we teach is not meant to suggest that teaching reading is a sterile, step-by-step endeavor; it just indicates that the teaching and learning of reading include many components.)

Within these learning experiences, when are we specifically teaching reading? I suggest that, while all these elements relate to making meaning of what one reads (they relate to students' learning to read), we are not *teaching reading* directly—we are teaching specific critical elements that contribute to a student's reading.

The same is true of teaching motivation. While we may not be directly teaching motivation, as with reading, we can teach specific critical elements that contribute to a student's motivation. Can we teach students to look, act, and be motivated? Of course we can. If students aren't motivated, that's not the end of the conversation—it should be the beginning. When a student seems unmotivated, educators should ask why that is the case and identify the most critical behavioral skills that have caused that lack of motivation. For example, if teachers observe students don't appear motivated (if they do not participate, ask questions, complete work, or behave enthusiastically), we should consider if they know how to:

- Pay attention in class
- Participate in learning experiences
- Complete homework

If students don't complete work, we should ask if they know how to:

- Manage their time
- Plan tasks

- Organize their materials
- Take and review notes

If students don't seem to know how to successfully learn (they do not take accurate notes, maintain organized binders and backpacks, or seem to know how to study for assessments), we should ask if they know how to:

- Set goals
- Delay gratification
- Practice self-discipline
- Persevere

If students don't work or interact well with peers and adults, we should ask if they know how to:

- Communicate socially
- Cooperate
- Consider others' points of view and feelings

If students don't seem to connect with others or to believe in themselves (they do not seem to be connected to peers, adults, or activities within the school, or they do not demonstrate that they have self-confidence), we should ask if they:

- Feel like they belong in the classroom and at the school
- Believe that they get smarter when they put forth effort
- See value in school and in learning
- Receive tasks with which they can succeed (tasks that are within their zone of proximal development)

Once we have identified the critical behavioral deficit, we can move on to defining and correcting the gap.

Define and Make Sense of These Skills

Just as collaborative teams define what mastery of academic learning targets looks like and sounds like, schools must describe in detail what mastery of behavioral skills looks like and sounds like. This is critical for two reasons.

1. Consistency of behavioral skill expectations is critical. When staff members possess a clear understanding of what students will do

and say when demonstrating these skills, consistency of reinforcing corrective feedback is much more likely.

2. Students and parents, who may not have been as involved in the identification of behavioral skill priorities, need to know the goals for which students are reaching.

Completing this step should follow the same processes that collaborative teams use when defining what mastery of prioritized academic skills looks and sounds like (some readers may know this process as determining the success criteria for identified learning targets). This step is simple and important: staff must clearly define success based on actions and words that can be observed when positive behaviors are displayed. *Behavior: The Forgotten Curriculum* (Weber, 2018) provides several examples.

Model, Teach, and Nurture These Skills

Recall the example of how we teach a student to read. It actually involves teaching several composite parts that work together to allow a student to read at fluency. Likewise, motivation is composed of several finite behavioral skills that work in tandem. The key to teaching motivation, then, lies in accurately modeling, teaching, and nurturing the problematic component part or parts with which the student is struggling.

If we provide environments and experiences that allow students to feel that they belong in academic communities; that their ability and competence grow with effort; that they can succeed; and that school has value for them, they will have growth mindsets and will be more likely to look, act, and be motivated.

If we model, teach, and nurture empathy, cooperation, self-advocacy, responsibility, and interpersonal skills, students will learn social skills and will be more likely to look, act, and be motivated.

If we model, teach, and nurture study skills, metacognition, self-regulation, and goal setting, students will develop learning strategies and will be more likely to look, act, and be motivated.

If we model, teach, and nurture grit, tenacity, delayed gratification, self-discipline, and self-control, students will develop perseverance and will be more likely to look, act, and be motivated.

If we model, teach, and nurture attendance, homework skills, organization, and participation, students will develop academic behaviors and will be more likely to look, act, and be motivated.

Perhaps we cannot directly teach motivation, but we can and must teach the antecedent skills and habits that lead to students' looking, acting, and being motivated.

When we fail to intentionally model, teach, and nurture these habits, we allow hopelessness to become an option. Chris Krebs (personal communication, February 14, 2019) recognizes the risks of not intentionally fostering behavioral skills:

> The most toxic thing that can happen to a school is when learning, success, and ambition are mocked and ridiculed by members of the student body. This climate is created when the community of adults, in both academia and the community at large, allows a sense of hopelessness to become the norm. Hopelessness is created when students fail to see the value in investing in their education, and feel external factors play a larger role in their future than their personal desires. Hopelessness breeds resentment toward those who are perceived as privileged, and ridicule toward those who appear naïve to the reality of their situation. Hopelessness is the single largest threat to the future of public schools.

Hopelessness need not hamper our students when there is a simple, common-sense solution. We must simply model, teach, and nurture behavioral skills the same way we do academic ones.

Measure Student Success in Displaying These Skills

Just as we gather evidence of students' academic progress, we must assess the extent to which students are meeting behavioral expectations. This evidence informs educators' success in nurturing these student skills and allows us to provide feedback and differentiated supports. *Behavior: The Forgotten Curriculum* (Weber, 2018) provides concrete tools that schools can use. I recommend starting with students' self-assessment of their progress. Collaborative teams can review these self-assessments to determine if students' evaluation of their current level of success matches their own.

Differentiate Supports That Respect Students' Readiness and Intervene When Needed

Just as in academics, there will be some students who need more time and alternative types of supports to be successful behaviorally. Let's be ready. When behavioral skills have been prioritized and mastery has been clearly defined, and when evidence of students' specific needs has been gathered and collaboratively analyzed, schoolwide teams and collaborative teams can respond with reteaching and intervention at any tier of support. *Behavior: The Forgotten Curriculum* (Weber, 2018) provides dozens of research-based strategies aligned to the behavioral categories determined as essential by educational psychologists (Farrington et al., 2012) as well as resources that can be used to determine which supports are most appropriate and plans to monitor the effectiveness of supports.

This six-step process to developing students' behavioral skills is actually effectively behavioral RTI. The process ensures that a system exists for predicting and preventing frustration instead of reacting to students' behavioral deficits. For example, we can predict students will bring very different, identifiable behavioral needs to our classrooms; we can prevent frustration and delay by being ready to model, teach, and measure these behaviors. We can predict that students will need differentiated supports to successfully access and demonstrate mastery of essential behavioral concepts and skills; we can proactively and positively prepare with varied teaching and learning options for Tier 1. We can predict that some students will learn at different rates and will need more than our first best instruction; we can then prepare with more time and alternative differentiated supports at planned regular intervals for students in Tier 2. We can predict that some students will have significant deficits in foundational skills; we can then prepare immediate, intensive, and targeted supports for those in Tier 3. In essence, behavioral RTI means actively and systematically anticipating students' behavioral needs and proactively preparing supports. When we implement the six steps of behavioral RTI correctly, we serve students in a timelier, more targeted, and more organized manner.

In addition to nurturing these skills, let's empower students, giving them a stake in their learning, teaching them responsibility, giving them responsibility, and holding them accountable for their learning. We can involve students in the processes of gathering evidence, getting and giving feedback, and relearning. We can also implement an alternative strategy to improving student motivation, which my district uses, known as the *empowerment mindset equation*.

Following the Empowerment Mindset Equation

In Irvine Unified School District, we use an empowerment mindset (EM) equation to focus on enhancing student empowerment and improving student mindsets. This equation is as follows:

$$EM = (relationships + rigor + relevance) + (student\ voice + choice + agency)$$

Here are a few examples of how the district boosts EM.

- **Making connections with the students:** We have accepted that students respond well to teachers they like; in effect, they won't care to know until they know we care. A student's sense of belonging increases when a school acts on the knowledge that relationships matter (Walton & Cohen, 2007, 2011; Yeager & Walton, 2011). Making connections with students is critical. It's common sense: when students are connected to something or someone on campus—when they feel like they belong—they are more committed and more engaged. Recognizing this common-sense truth, we set the big, hairy, audacious goal (BHAG; Collins & Porras, 2004) that every student have a connection to something and someone at school, whether it be a person, a sport, a band, or a club.

- **Promoting more positive student and staff mindsets:** Consider these previously described growth mindset statements (page 77). We are developing action plans that include the following concrete steps for promoting more positive student and staff mindsets.

    - *"I belong in this academic community."* To increase students' connections to school, we are reinvigorating advisory periods in secondary schools and classroom meetings in elementary schools. Classroom teachers, or the staff who serve as advisors to a group of students across their middle or high school careers, are tracking interactions within classrooms to ensure that a conversation (however brief) happens with every student at least every week. We are expanding the quantity and types of school activities or clubs so that every student can be involved, and we are holding students accountable for staying involved in and connected to something on campus. We are fully including all students, including students with special needs, in college preparatory courses, which two credentialed teachers typically co-teach.

    - *"My ability and competence grow with my effort."* To increase student and staff beliefs that, given time and the right supports, all students can learn at high levels, several collaborative teams no longer assign points to assessments before they return them, instead highlighting errors (opportunities for improvement) that they expect all students to correct or improve. Several teams no longer assign zeros, which either condemn students to a low grade or effectively let them off the hook. Instead, these teams assign incompletes and require students to complete all assignments that were worthy of being assigned in the first place. We are increasingly requiring students to refine assignments and retake tests on which they show less than the agreed-on level of mastery, instead of denying them the opportunity to show us what they now know after correcting errors, relearning concepts, and receiving support. We are more consistently communicating a "not yet" approach to lack of understanding, as in, "I don't get this yet," instead of, "I don't get this." Finally, we are making more of an effort to ensure that we explicitly learn from errors; we use routines like *My Favorite No*, in which a teacher shares a "good" mistake with the class as an opportunity to grow. A good mistake is typically one from a solution in which much was done correctly but a pivotal, significant step was missed; reflecting upon, analyzing, and correcting these errors proactively addresses misconceptions.

- *"I can succeed at this."* To increase students' and staff's beliefs that success with a task is possible, we have acknowledged that we do not know enough about what differentiating and scaffolding are and how to do them. Differentiation strategies are now shared and modeled at all professional learning events; and we have a long way to go. We are differentiating content and processes so that all students can access grade-level and course-specific concepts. We are providing students with multiple ways of showing what they know (for example, by recording their responses as a video, a screencast, or audio).

- *"This work has value for me."* To increase the relevance and purpose that students see in schools, learning, and tasks, we are striving to design experiences that tap into students' lives. In addition, we are working to individualize supports at all tiers, promoting more voice, choice, and agency so we increase the value that students place on their learning. We are listening to students' voices and using their input when providing options for the content with which they engage, the processes they use for learning, the products they use to show what they know, and the needs that they have. We are increasing choice, allowing students to exercise some agency over the place, pace, path, and time of day that they learn. We are striving to increase agency, giving students a stake in their learning, and inviting (or requiring) them to track their progress toward learning.

- **Creating a behavioral curriculum:** Portola High School in Irvine Unified School District has specified the behavioral skills that all students will develop, with the specific performance levels required in grades 9–10 and grades 11–12. These skills are explicitly taught during advisory periods and embedded into academic courses and tasks by teacher advisors. The skills are as follows: taking risks, self-advocating, utilizing resources, adapting, organizing and prioritizing, inquiring, innovating, synthesizing, evaluating, researching effectively, being digitally literate, creating and defending a claim, speaking and writing clearly and compellingly, reading complex texts purposefully and insightfully, collaborating, serving, positively and actively participating, honoring norms, and acknowledging others.

  John Pehrson (personal communication, February 13, 2019), the principal of this school, notes:

  > These skills need to be seen as more important than they are. More than words on a page, they need to be referred to early and often by teachers across all disciplines. If collaboration is an important skill for all graduates to master, it needs to be practiced in all disciplines often. In addition, it needs to be modeled and assessed so that it can be improved upon each time. By emphasizing specific skills by name across all disciplines, students are able to draw connections more easily. Something as simple as listing the skills with descriptions under each, and then asking kids to self-assess their own competency level, makes it evident to them what they need to focus on and helps each student to see what skills they need the most help in developing.

  If we want students to internalize and display these skills, we must actually make them visible within teaching and learning—that's just common sense.

- **Providing explicit instruction on behavioral skills:** One of the elementary schools with which I have worked, Saffel Street Elementary School in Lawrenceburg, Kentucky, starts the day with fifteen minutes of instruction of behavioral skills. The school's motto is "Reaching for the stars," so staff call these fifteen minutes in the morning the *launchpad*. A team of staff members wrote lesson plans that all teachers use for this instruction, and two staff members are in each room during launchpad: the classroom teacher and a support staff member (support staff include custodial staff, administrators, and classified staff). On Mondays, staff and students define the skill and corresponding expectations. On Tuesdays, students complete a graphic organizer to make sense of and dive deeper into the skill. On Wednesdays, teachers show a story or video to identify examples and nonexamples of the skill. On Thursdays, students act out, role-play, or write about the skill. Last, on Fridays, classes celebrate specific successes from throughout the week in displaying the skill and provide feedback. The skills that this school has prioritized are respect, responsibility, cooperation, empathy, perseverance, integrity, engagement, and self-belief. They introduce or revisit topics each week throughout the year.

- **Using learning target trackers:** A fundamental foundation of our EM equation is the learning target tracker, described in great detail in chapter 4 (page 59), in the area of agency. I interpret agency as when a teacher provides a student with a significant role to play in their learning journey. Trackers give students such a role and responsibility.

Believing Educators Can Motivate Students

Here's another common-sense notion: students will be motivated when we, as leaders and staff, believe that we have the ability to motivate them. Hattie (2019) calls this concept *collective teacher efficacy*, and defines it as follows:

> Collective teacher efficacy (CTE) is the collective belief of the staff of the school/faculty in their ability to positively affect students. CTE has been found to be strongly, positively correlated to student achievement. A school staff that believes that it can collectively achieve great things is vital for the health of a school, and if they believe that they can make a positive difference then they very likely will.

Of the 252 indicators that John Hattie (2019) has studied, Hattie has found that collective teacher efficacy has the greatest positive impact on student achievement, with an effect size of 1.57. The importance of believing you can have an effect cannot be overstated.

Students know when educators have high expectations for their success (Zimmerman et al., 1992). When educators have high expectations, students learn at higher levels. Educators can make no references to *that student* or *those students*. They can allow no label to persuade them that students cannot self-regulate, be motivated, or cooperate. With proactive and positive supports, educators can make significant progress, and they can get all students on track (or back on track) for college, career, and future readiness. Researchers have found that behavioral skills are malleable (Farrington et al., 2012), and the educators with whom I have worked have experienced it.

Schools implementing behavioral RTI sometimes believe that the teaching, modeling, and nurturing of behavioral skills is only for "naughty" students, students at risk, or students from historically underperforming subgroups. This could not be further from the truth. All students will benefit from developing more effective behavioral skills. Too often, behavioral RTI efforts (and academic RTI efforts, for that matter) only focus on intervention, or Tiers 2 and 3. Having a Tier 1 focus means that all students receive supports in the behavioral skills needed for success in school, college, career, and life. All means *all*. We have met high-achieving students who do not persevere, and gifted students with fixed mindsets. Schools need not worry about when they will pull vulnerable students to teach them behavioral skills; they should already have the time built in. The teaching and learning of behavioral skills is for all, and must be part of every school's core Tier 1 environments.

Some educators may feel that a focus on behavioral skills is now unnecessary, given the increasing popularity of facilitated learning experiences, project-based learning, the maker movement, and competency-based education (Colby, 2017; Dougherty & Conrad, 2016; Larmer, Mergendoller, & Boss, 2015). In other words, perhaps more contemporary pedagogies and practices (present in a growing number of future-ready schools) already represent the answer to the question, How do we nurture behavioral skills within students? They very well may, but while next-generation teaching may be more facilitative and learning may be more experiential, students still need to get guidance, to see adults modeling good habits, and to receive behavioral skills instruction. As Farrington and colleagues (2012) report:

> Students are not likely to develop learning strategies in the absence either of explicit instruction or classwork that requires the use of such strategies. It may be most helpful to think about noncognitive factors as properties of the interactions between students and classrooms or school environments. Rather than being helpless in the face of students who lack perseverance and good academic behaviors, teachers set the classroom conditions that strongly shape the nature of students' academic performance.
>
> The essential question is not how to change students to improve their behavior but rather how to create contexts that better support students in developing critical attitudes and learning strategies necessary for their academic success. Thus, teaching adolescents to become learners may require educators to shift their own beliefs and practices as well as to build their pedagogical skills and strategies to support student learning in new ways. Academic behaviors and perseverance

may need to be thought of as creations of school and classroom contexts rather than as personal qualities that students bring with them to school. (p. 72)

So how do educators do it? What silver bullet or magic formula will help teachers and schools help students develop these habits? There may be unique strategies about which educators do not know. But the practices that will likely help students develop critical behavioral skills are the very same research-based best practices that educators have read about but have not found time to implement, or have not implemented well. These include rigorous and relevant teaching, collaborative learning, and differentiated instruction, to name a few.

Conclusion

We cannot simply view motivation as the cause of student difficulties. When a student does not act or appear motivated, we must analyze the causes of the apparent apathy and take steps to address these antecedents. And we must give ourselves grace; most educators did not receive information on nurturing students' behavioral skills within their preservice training, and guiding the development of these skills was not seen as the responsibility of schools. Two critical facts have changed. First, there is clear research and guidance on what behaviors are most critical for students to possess and proof that they are malleable. Second, it's clear that behavioral skills are as critical to success in school, college, career, and life as academic skills. It's common sense: if students do not possess these skills, we must teach these skills.

We must also gather evidence of students' progress toward fully developing these skills, habits, and attributes. Gathering such evidence and providing feedback for all student outcomes are the topics of the next chapter.

Next Steps

Please complete the following next steps as you consider changes that may be appropriate for your school or district as you address the root causes of motivation.

1. Examine current practices by considering the following questions.

    - To what extent do staff use student apathy, or a lack of student motivation, to excuse staff members' lack of success in ensuring that all students learn at high levels?

    - How comprehensively do staff, students, and parents understand the school's behavioral expectations and those skills students need for success in school, college, career, and life?

    - How do the five domains of behavioral skills described in this chapter (mindsets, social skills, perseverance, learning strategies, and academic behaviors; page 76) match your expected set of behavioral priorities? How could you embed a few elements that the research defines into your existing list?

    - To what extent do teachers explicitly teach behavioral skills to all students? Do they teach them on a regular (at least weekly) basis?

    - To what extent do teachers embed the modeling, teaching, reinforcing, and practicing of behavioral skills into academic lessons, tasks, and activities? Do they do it on a regular (at least weekly) basis?

    - How do teachers gather, measure, and assess evidence regarding all students' success in learning and displaying behavioral skills?

    - How do teachers give feedback to all students regarding behavioral skills, both students successfully exhibiting these skills and students not yet displaying these skills?

2. Discover research- and evidence-based common-sense practices by doing the following.

    - Use the domains of behavioral skills described in this chapter (mindsets, social skills, perseverance, learning strategies, and academic behaviors; page 76) to diagnose or determine why a student isn't acting motivated or displaying appropriate behavioral skills.

    - Compare your existing list of behavioral skill priorities with the five domains identified in the research, and make slight adjustments to your lists as you deem necessary.

Doing What Works © 2020 Solution Tree Press • SolutionTree.com
Visit **go.SolutionTree.com/leadership** to download this free reproducible.

- Craft learning targets from the behavioral skills that you have prioritized to share with students and inform teaching, learning, and assessment.

- Explicitly teach a behavioral skill once a week during a fifteen-minute minilesson at the beginning of the day (in elementary school) or in first period, advisory, or homeroom (in secondary school). You can use the same lesson, with slight adjustments for student age, across the school.

- Reinforce behavioral skill practice (of the target skill for the week or month) within academic lessons, tasks, and activities, using strategies presented in chapter 5 at least once a week.

- Quickly and efficiently gather evidence of students' success in learning and displaying behavioral skills, perhaps starting with students' self-assessments of their success in exhibiting behavioral skills.

- Dedicate PLC at Work time to collaboratively analyzing evidence of students' behavioral skill success and collectively determining the necessary differentiated supports.

3. Identify what you will stop doing, and develop a stop-doing plan.

4. Identify what you will start doing, and develop a start-doing plan.

6

Fostering Two-Way Feedback

If someone asked educators why we assess, and we responded honestly, I believe that most educators would say, "To give points and to assign a grade." This is what the *of* refers to in the expression *assessment* of *learning* (Stiggins, 2006). We must continue to transform our assessment practices toward assessment *for* learning and even to assessment *as* learning (see chapter 4, page 59).

In the mid-20th century, David Ausubel (1968) wrote one of the most common sense of all truths in the epigraph of the seminal *Educational Psychology: A Cognitive View*: "The most important single factor influencing learning is what the learner already knows. Ascertain this and teach him accordingly" (p. iv). We cannot do this common-sense work without knowing where students are. We cannot do this work without intentionally and frequently embedding opportunities for students to give us feedback.

When we gather evidence, students are giving us feedback about where they are and what they need to keep learning. We can, in turn, give students feedback on what they're doing well and where they still have room for growth, and we can begin to partner in the next steps toward continuous improvement.

It's common sense—assessment provides the opportunity to get and give feedback. Feedback is a two-way street. To illustrate the importance of this chapter's common-sense leadership practice, the following sections will detail educational practices that defy common sense, research-based best practices in education, and strategies and insights for improving student learning.

Educational Practices That Defy Common Sense

Giving "feedback" through points and percentages not only threatens mindsets (see chapter 6, page 95) but also is inaccurate. Consider a constructed-response test made up of ten items, each worth three points. If a student earns two out of three on each item, meaning the student had the right idea and even the correct process but did not arrive at the one correct answer, he or she earns twenty out of thirty points, or 67 percent—a D grade. Are the points, percentage, and letter grade representative of what the student knows? More importantly, do they provide students the feedback they need to keep learning (assuming that we give them the opportunity to keep learning)? Does two out of three, or twenty out of thirty, give us the feedback we need from a student to know what the student knows and does not yet know? Do these portions of points guide us in how to help the student improve? The answer to all these questions is a clear, resounding *no*.

Likewise, it surprises us when students stop trying or become frustrated during a grading period when they earn an F on an early test—let's say a 40 percent. Yet, if they earned an 80 percent on each of the three other tests within the semester, their final grade would at best be a low C, assuming they earned 100 percent on every other test. Does that accurately represent their understanding? Should it surprise us if the hope of a C doesn't inspire them to persevere? Do we provide students with feedback on why they earned that first grade, allow them the opportunity (or even require them) to learn what they didn't learn, and give them the chance (or, again, require them) to show us what they now know? If the content, skills, and concepts were important enough to teach and assess, aren't they important enough for us to allow or even require multiple opportunities to learn them?

We cannot simply state that we taught the content and they didn't learn it. We may lament that students do not have growth mindsets, viewing their learning as fixed and neglecting to sufficiently persevere, yet we may not give them opportunities to say, "I haven't learned it yet, but I may if I continue to put forth effort." We do not allow them to practice a growth mindset.

We lament that students are not engaged in their learning, yet we do not provide them the feedback they need to know where they currently are and where they need to go. We hand back assignments, quizzes, tests, and projects with points, percentages, and pen marks and expect them to take responsibility for learning and for determining what they need to do.

Two of the three big ideas of PLC at Work are a focus on learning and a focus on results (DuFour et al., 2016). To meet the spirit of these two ideas, we must more frequently gather feedback on where students are. Determining what students know at the end of a unit (summative assessment) is simply too late. A *focus on learning* means we know how we are doing in helping students learn, and how students are doing at learning, on a frequent, at least daily, basis. Likewise, we cannot leave our *focus on results* to results on end-of-unit assessments. Yes, we can gain great insights from these common assessments (and we can learn as professionals within a community of colleagues), but we must gather more frequent and accurate feedback from students on what they know, and give more feedback to students on where they are.

At the very least, let's accept that assessment and grading are not the same thing. And let's commit to assessment—to evidence gathering—as a way of getting *and giving* feedback. That's the common-sense need and opportunity of assessment.

Research-Based Best Practices in Education

Like David Ausubel, Benjamin Bloom launched a half century of research that consistently reports the very high effect size of formative assessments (Bloom, Hastings, & Madaus, 1971). He reports that, following high-quality initial instruction, teachers' administration of a formative assessment helps identify "precisely what students have learned well and where they still need additional work" (Guskey, 2010, p. 53). These assessments provide feedback on where students are in their learning journey, to both students and teachers. Of course, as chapter 2 (page 31) described, Bloom's research on assessments that inform future teaching and learning also demonstrates the efficacy of response to intervention, the larger system that he designed and studied. Consider the term *response* within response to instruction and response to intervention—we gather feedback on how students are *responding*, and we use that feedback to *respond* to the needs that emerge.

Tom Guskey (2005), assessment expert and preeminent Bloom scholar, further makes this connection when describing the most common-sense use of assessment:

> A far better approach, according to Bloom, would be for teachers to use their classroom assessments as learning tools, and then to follow those assessments with a *feedback and corrective* procedure. In other words, instead of using assessments only as evaluation devices that mark the end of each unit, Bloom recommended using them as part of the instructional process to *diagnose* individual learning difficulties (feedback) and to *prescribe* remediation procedures (correctives).

The notion of assessment that provides feedback is not new, and it's connected to the systems of supports that all students deserve—and that some students need to learn at high levels, given that not all students learn concepts the first time, and others come to a new grade level with significant needs in foundational skills.

Formative assessment means that we gather evidence that *informs* where we are and what we still need to do. The evidence provides us feedback and allows us to provide feedback. Consider Michael Fullan's (2005) words on this topic:

> Assessment for learning . . . when done well . . . is one of the most powerful high-leverage strategies for improving student learning that we know of. Educators collectively at the school and district levels become more skilled and focused at assessing, disaggregating, and using student achievement as a tool for ongoing improvement. (p. 71)

For assessment, or evidence gathering, to be good for more than assigning a grade—for it to be a "tool for ongoing improvement"—we need to accept student performance on assessments as feedback, and we need to intentionally use assessment results to provide feedback to students.

Earlier chapters have described Lev Vygotsky's contributions to education in social and active learning. Of course, he also researched the significance of meeting students where they are, as did David Ausubel (1968) fifty years later, defining a student's zone of proximal development as "The distance between the actual developmental level as determined by independent problem solving and the level of potential development as determined through problem solving under adult guidance or in collaboration with more capable peers" (as cited in Vygotsky, 1978, p. 86).

We can only determine these distances and locate students' zone of proximal development by gathering feedback regarding where they are right now.

John Hattie and Helen Timperley (2007) make direct connections between evidence gathering and feedback:

> Feedback has no effect in a vacuum; to be powerful in its effect, there must be a learning context to which feedback is addressed. It is but part of the teaching process and is that which happens second—after a student has responded to initial instruction—when information is provided regarding some aspect(s) of the student's task performance. It is most powerful when it addresses faulty interpretations, not a total lack of understanding. Under the latter circumstance, it may even be threatening to a student. (p. 82)

In common-sense terms, our feedback to students should give information about where they are going, how they are going, and where they need to go next. Hattie and Timperley's (2007) work is considered the definitive study of this critical and common-sense idea, and states the necessity of two-way feedback surrounding assessment:

> There are many ways in which teachers can deliver feedback to students and for students to receive feedback from teachers, peers, and other sources. The implication is not that we should automatically use more tests. Rather, for students, it means gaining information about how and what they understand and misunderstand, finding directions and strategies that they must take to improve, and seeking assistance to understand the goals of the learning. For teachers, it means devising activities and questions that provide feedback to them about the effectiveness of their teaching, particularly so they know what to do next. Assessments can perform all these feedback functions, but too often, they are devoid of effective feedback to students or to teachers. (pp. 101–102)

It's common sense: students give us feedback on how we've done in teaching, and then we give them feedback on how they're doing. Following this, as research from chapter 2 (page 31) validates, we should be ready with supports that we base on that feedback to continue the learning.

Strategies and Insights for Improving Student Learning

Feedback as a two-way street is not purely about what educators and students communicate directly to each other. Often, the most effective feedback comes via assessment. Unfortunately, educators may have become jaded about this critical but complicated topic in the teaching-learning process. We must have evidence, by way of assessment, but we face a paradox—many educators believe that they assess too much, yet they do not possess the information they require to inform their work. Educators may also feel that they do not have time for assessments (Weber, 2013).

We should know what to do to gather and give feedback. After all, it's what PLCs do. According to noted assessment author Cassandra Erkens, "The best way to improve schools involves functioning as collaborative teams that use evidence to make informed decisions that ultimately support all students leading to high levels of achievement" (C. Erkens, personal communication, October 18, 2018). Common evidence-gathering opportunities give teams the feedback (from students) that they need to learn with and from one another, collectively responding to questions such as:

- "Who has not yet learned the prioritized standards in the unit?"
- "For what specific standards, and learning targets within these standards, must the teacher devote more time and employ different approaches?"

- "Which teacher on the team has had the most relative success with these standards and skills?"
- "If there is not a teacher on the team who has had more success, do we have teachers within the broader school system whom we can contact?"
- "What external resources, strategies, or professional development can we access?"

These questions are the foundation of a PLC at Work. Without frequent and common evidence-gathering opportunities, we simply won't have feedback from students about how we've done, and where students are, to inform the feedback that we will give and the supports that we will provide.

This section will describe several strategies that can assist educators facing the conundrum of how to best gather evidence and provide and receive effective feedback. It will discuss:

- Assessing assessments
- Considering preassessments
- Embracing assessment as learning
- Encouraging students to take responsibility for their learning
- Providing reassessment opportunities
- Finding time for feedback
- Passing feedback upward

As always, words of encouragement and wisdom from teachers in the field will accompany these strategies.

Assessing Assessments

Receiving feedback via assessments has the key advantage that it allows educators to be more instructionally agile—to differentiate teaching and learning. Cassandra Erkens believes that:

> In order for individual teachers to become instructionally agile, they must be precise yet flexible as they make instructional maneuvers based on emerging evidence. Precision requires that teachers operate with a set of shared expectations in their classrooms, and flexibility requires that teachers apply targeted instructional responses to address gaps in student understanding within short periods of time. (C. Erkens, personal communication, October 18, 2018)

Cassandra Erkens argues that teaching without assessment cannot really be called *instruction*:

> Teaching without evidence to inform instruction is the equivalent of engaging in curriculum coverage. Worse, if the curriculum being covered doesn't have shared agreements (e.g., a guaranteed and viable curriculum) among staff, then students are subjected to discrete teaching (teachers can select their own topics/areas of focus) and learning that is contingent on what their teachers chose. (C. Erkens, personal communication, October 18, 2018)

Instruction and assessment have an inextricable link; checks for understanding and observations count as evidence and feedback, and can inform feedback and future instruction.

All educators should begin their journey toward two-way feedback by inventorying the assessments that they are currently administering. When assessing your current assessments, look for several things by asking yourself the following questions.

- "Am I gathering timely information to ensure that all students learn at high levels?"
- "Am I gathering this information without redundancies and inefficiencies?"
- "Does the information I receive help me decide whether to move on, slow down, or reteach the content—in other words, does it help my instructional agility?"
- "Do I conduct quick, formative checks for student understanding as well as summative assessments?"

As you answer these questions, decide whether you should keep, discard, or rewrite your current assessments in order to better meet your goals.

Further, in my experience, the feedback that we receive from students is sometimes a bit inaccurate because, too often, we do not assess standards or learning targets; we assess *activities*. In other words, we do not base the points that we give a paper, the percentage we give a mathematics test, or the letter grade we give a lab on student mastery of standards; rather, we base it on student success on the activity. In Irvine Unified School District, we are confronting this reality as we assess our assessments, and striving to ensure that our activities and tests assess standards. Our initial steps have been to map out the number and purposes of assessment that we administer within an instructional unit, to ensure that assessment items match the agreed-on meaning (success criteria) of the standards (or learning targets) that we are striving to ensure that all students learn, and to embed time after the administration of assessments to provide reteaching and enrichment supports.

Considering Preassessments

Evidence-gathering opportunities like screening and preassessment, when done well, can actually *save* instructional time. Screening reveals which students have significant deficits that will almost certainly cause them to experience difficulties at some time and in some content area during the year. Immediately initiating supports saves time and preserves students' belief in their own efficacy. Preassessing reveals students who have gaps in their knowledge of immediate prerequisite skills—"gaps that will likely necessitate interventions within the unit" (Weber, 2013).

Educators should preteach prerequisites—for which they have evidence that a need exists—before and at the beginning of units so they fill gaps, prepare their students for success, and minimize the need to spend time on interventions later. This will, of course, require that time is allocated for preteaching, but it will need to be allocated before, during, or after units, or some students will be left behind. We can predict it. Preassessments can also reveal that students already possess knowledge of upcoming units' content. By compacting content, educators can avoid wasting time on content students already understand, "thereby allowing time for more depth of study or more practice with other content" (Weber, 2013).

Embracing Assessment as Learning

Irvine Unified School District is embracing assessment *as* learning, moving beyond assessment *of* and *for* learning. Assessment as learning occurs when the process of and actions of assessment actually directly impact and improve learning. I have already described some strategies we are using for this purpose, including our efforts to empower students (see chapter 3, page 47) and our use of learning target trackers (see chapter 4, page 59). For educators and students to view assessments as opportunities to learn, educators must give timely and targeted feedback to students. The quality of this feedback to students will depend on the quality of the feedback that educators gather. The better educators craft learning targets, and the better they determine success criteria, the better chance they have of crafting quality assessments and therefore gaining quality feedback from students about what they do and do not yet know. This in turn will allow educators to provide timely, specific, and actionable feedback to students.

Encouraging Students to Take Responsibility for Their Learning

Irvine Unified School District is increasingly requiring (not simply allowing) students to take responsibility for their learning. For example, our teachers are using a strategy called *highlight grading*, sometimes known as *dot grading*. The concept is simple enough: when assessing an assignment or test, the teacher highlights (or makes dots next to) a portion of student work that requires attention—perhaps a process, solution, or explanation is incorrect or incomplete. That's it—that's the initial feedback to the student. It indicates that the unhighlighted portions of the assignment or test have met expectations. Students must then analyze the highlighted portions and make improvements, either individually or with peers, or in coaching sessions with the teacher (during which the teacher does not provide answers). Once the student resubmits the assignment or test, the teacher only assesses the previously highlighted parts and records a grade. This method reinforces a growth mindset and is a common-sense way of giving feedback and requiring students to do something with it. An interesting and important note on highlight grading is that teachers write neither points nor percentages on returned assignments and assessments; it has surprised and pleased our teachers that neither students nor parents seem to mind this.

Providing Reassessment Opportunities

Aside from highlight grading, our teachers are also very creatively exploring ways that allow, and even require, students to recomplete work and retake assessments when they have not yet achieved mastery. This is not an original idea, but it does address a question that students will logically ask: "What's in it for me if I use a teacher's feedback to improve my work?" It's wonderful to think that students will naturally and independently re-engage with concepts that they have not yet learned. But it defies common sense to believe that they will do so if they do not have the opportunity to reassess—to give us new feedback on where they are, while we give them new feedback on what they know now—and improve their grade.

Reassessing is a logical, common-sense practice. It communicates to students, "We expect you to use the feedback to relearn and then show us what you know now." But reassessment has raised the issue of fairness. Some teachers believe that it is not fair to students who passed a test the first time when we allow other students multiple opportunities to take the test. And some teachers feel that allowing these multiple opportunities does not teach responsibility (Weber, 2013).

We all have an important decision to make, because a firm commitment to giving students only one chance to demonstrate their learning entirely contradicts a firm commitment to helping all students learn at high levels. As parents, caregivers, or teachers, we all recognize that children rarely learn at the same rate and in the same manner, and "to terminate instruction at an arbitrary date and suggest that learning of that content is at an end, and the one-time opportunity to demonstrate mastery is upon us," defies common sense (Weber, 2013).

But what about teaching responsibility? Educators in Irvine Unified School District believe demanding that students persevere until they succeed teaches responsibility more effectively than giving them only one chance to do so. What do we teach students when we communicate that they don't actually have to learn the content once they've failed that first test—"that they are off the hook and need not keep trying"? (Weber, 2013).

We do more to teach responsibility when we demand that students keep up with the new concepts *and* receive additional support on the old concepts until they reach the level of understanding they need to be successful. When we allow reassessment, we are teaching perseverance; we are insisting that they learn how to learn, and continuously strive to improve (Weber, 2013).

High school mathematics teacher Matthew Beyranevand has inspired Irvine Unified School District's reassessment work. Beyranevand is the author of the blog *Math With Matthew*, a Global Math Project ambassador, the K–12 mathematics department coordinator for Chelmsford Public Schools in Massachusetts, a member of the Massachusetts STEM Advisory Council, and the author of *Teach Math Like This, Not Like That* (Beyranevand, 2017b). His blog post "Retaking Assessments: Many Math Teachers Are Late to the Party!" (Beyranevand, 2017a) starts with a belief to which I wholeheartedly subscribe: all assessments can and should be formative. That means we should use the feedback that we get from the evidence students provide to inform future instruction and to provide feedback to students. The concepts in the next unit almost always build on the concepts in the last unit. By not committing to relearning and reassessment, we pretty obviously set students and ourselves up for failure.

Beyranevand (2017a) starts his reassessment process by assigning students a reflection ticket, which requires them to reflect on why they made errors. Teachers in Irvine Unified School District use various forms of exam wrappers and test correction processes that achieve the same goal: they require students to identify the learning target with which they need support and begin to analyze why they missed the target. Beyranevand then requires students to seek and receive assistance. Each district school has tutorial times (see chapter 2, page 31) within which students can receive this support. We are also increasingly assigning Khan Academy lessons (www.khanacademy.org; and lessons through related personalized online tools) with which students can engage in targeted relearning. Beyranevand (2017a) also requires that students complete any and all missing work from the unit. Then, the teacher will administer a new assessment to any student who scored 20 to 90 percent on the first attempt. And importantly, the new grade is the new grade—no averaging. District teachers follow very similar procedures, striving for both success and sustainability. Though there may be bumps along the way, we are committed to finding a solution; we won't go back to traditional one-chance methods.

Finding Time for Feedback

Timely and targeted feedback is the goal, and we recognize that it makes sense that it will enhance learning, but how do we find the time for it? Irvine Unified School District teachers are empowering students' peers to provide the feedback. The process is simple: First, develop and share a simple scoring guide or rubric. Then, ask students to identify a positive attribute of their classmates' work. Next, have students provide constructive, positively worded suggestions for continuous improvement. Providing this kind of feedback is a skill that you must teach and they must practice. Our teachers have found that peer feedback is most effective when it focuses on a specific aspect of the task, such as the quality of evidence in science or social studies, the quality of explanations in mathematics, or the effectiveness of transitions in writing.

Of course, having teachers provide written feedback and rubric-based feedback is effective, but it requires a lot of time. So, let's apply common sense: To how much feedback can students reasonably respond? Our teachers have adopted the one-item feedback model. Teachers give feedback on one element of the assignment, and they expect students to make improvements related to this one element. One element does not mean one item; it may be the use of commas in writing, the organization of supporting work in mathematics, or the amount of evidence used to justify a claim in multiple content areas.

Passing Feedback Upward

One last common-sense idea on feedback relates to passing feedback upward. By the end of a semester or school year, students have given us a lot of feedback. What if teachers systematically recorded this evidence and forwarded this feedback upward to next semester's or next year's teachers? How much more prepared would we be to support all students to success through scaffolds and differentiated supports? How much earlier in the year could we provide intensive supports when feedback from the prior year reveals significant needs? This is a low-cost, highly effective form of universal screening, and it can and should inform proactively prepared Tier 1 instruction and Tier 3 intervention. It's common sense, and it's based on feedback that students give to us—and, in this case, feedback that we give to our colleagues.

Conclusion

Assessments—big and small, simple and complex, formal and informal—are events during which students give us feedback. Irvine Unified School District is committed to more accurately and intentionally gathering that feedback and to, in turn, giving students feedback about where they are and what they need to do to grow. And we're giving them the time and support to make the growth and the opportunities to show us how they've made the growth. Cassie Parham (personal communication, November 14, 2019), Irvine Unified School District's assistant superintendent of instructional services, believes that instruction is best and learning most likely to occur when teachers design the instruction to meet student needs:

> When we use evidence to inform our instruction, we can tailor instruction to meet the needs of our learners. We can ensure that every student masters the essential learning outcomes, and provide the additional support or enrichment that they need to be successful. We know that all students don't learn at the same rate or in the same way, so we need to use evidence to determine how to intervene to ensure that they all succeed at the highest levels. Using evidence to inform teaching and learning helps educators provide instruction that is targeted, meaningful, and just in time.
>
> We would never stand for a doctor diagnosing without evidence or providing treatment that wasn't targeted and appropriate. Teaching shouldn't be any different. We can't simply teach lessons that we assume will meet our students' needs. First, we need to marshal evidence to understand their needs. We should be using evidence to guide every instructional decision.

We can only meet student needs when we have the timely and targeted evidence required to know and respond to those needs.

We cannot limit the feedback that we gather and give to the mere acquisition of content knowledge. Students must be able to use the content knowledge that they acquire. Skills are as important as or more important than content knowledge. This common-sense idea will be the topic of the next chapter.

Next Steps

Please complete the following next steps as you consider changes that may be appropriate for your school or district to improve two-way feedback.

1. Examine current practices by considering the following questions.
   - To what extent do educators give students timely, explicit feedback when they gather evidence (administer assessments) of student learning?
   - How might the school conduct an assessment inventory to look for redundancies or gaps, as well as determine whether it assesses too much?
   - To what extent do teachers use assessment information and collective analyses of student learning to inform future teaching and learning?
   - To what extent do teachers use assessment information and collective analyses of student learning to inform Tier 2 enrichment and intervention (see chapter 2, page 31)?
   - In what ways are students involved in the evidence-gathering process?
   - In what ways do grades on tests, tasks, and activities communicate to students where they are in terms of specific learning targets, why they are where they are, and what they need to do to improve?
   - To what extent do educators view assessments (of all kinds) as feedback from students regarding students' needs and educators' success?
   - To what extent do teachers limit "feedback" to assigning points and percentages and marking incorrect responses?

2. Discover research- and evidence-based common-sense practices by doing the following.
   - Consider inventorying your current assessments, eliminating redundancies, and striving to ensure that almost all assessments (evidence-gathering opportunities) are followed by dedicated time during which students can act on the feedback they receive.
   - Consider *not* assessing or grading everything.
   - Brainstorm ways in which students can be more involved in the assessment and feedback process, from assessing themselves to assessing their peers to taking responsibility for their learning through the use of learning target trackers.
   - Ensure that assessments and assessment items specifically measure mastery of standards and targets, and not simply an overall grade on an assignment or test.

page 1 of 2

Doing What Works © 2020 Solution Tree Press • SolutionTree.com
Visit **go.SolutionTree.com/leadership** to download this free reproducible.

- Consider exploring and implementing standards-based grading principles and practices. (Hint: You do not need to get rid of letter grades on report cards.)
- Consider engaging in professional learning opportunities to learn efficient and effective ways of getting and giving feedback.
- Embed feedback opportunities into unit plans.
- Rededicate teams' focus to the four critical questions of PLC at Work.
- Systematically use feedback (data) to make timely and targeted programmatic adjustments to students' educational paths.

3. Identify what you will stop doing, and develop a stop-doing plan.

4. Identify what you will start doing, and develop a start-doing plan.

7

Emphasizing Skills Alongside or Above Content

In chapter 1 (page 15), I made a common-sense case for how much we should teach. In chapter 3 (page 47), I suggested common-sense strategies for how we should teach. In the next chapter (page 125), I'll describe common-sense ways to enhance the rigor of what we teach. In this chapter, we'll explore the importance of balance in what we teach.

Content, and the acquisition of content knowledge, is not enough. The skills, habits, attributes, and dispositions that students employ when interacting with content knowledge are critically important; they always have been. However, now more than ever, education has renewed recognition and renewed requirements that reasoning skills receive at least as much attention in learning experiences as the acquisition of content knowledge.

If we want students to remember and retain skills and knowledge, to apply and make connections, and to find relevance and be engaged, then their learning experiences must reflect the common-sense notion that skills are as important as, or more important than, content. To illustrate the importance of this chapter's common-sense leadership practice, the following sections will detail educational practices that defy common sense, research-based best practices in education, and strategies and insights for improving student learning.

Educational Practices That Defy Common Sense

Teachers teach what they are asked to teach; the curriculum that they most commonly taught before 2010, for better or worse, reflected the standards in place up until that year. Before 2010, schools expected teachers to raise test scores on high-stakes, statewide tests that measured low-level knowledge. Many schools, understandably, planned backward from these tests. Learning the formula, the procedure, the algorithm, and the rule became the end goal. This resulted in educators' favoring memorization and basic levels of content acquisition in curriculum, instruction, and assessment.

Ironically, this approach to raising test scores most decidedly did not work—certainly not for me or the other educators in schools and school districts in which I have worked. In fact, it was only when educators in the school in which I was a principal, and districts in which I worked at the central office, embedded opportunities for students to apply skills, beginning most comprehensively in 2005, that student learning exploded, and yes, test scores increased (Buffum et al., 2009).

Not only high-stakes tests emphasized content over skills. Rigid pacing guides and curriculum maps also discouraged learning in depth, using content knowledge, and applying skills. How did they do this? These guides and maps were (and are) typically tied to textbooks, and low-level content acquisition dominates lessons in textbooks. In addition, maps and guides too often were (and are) packed with a new lesson for every day. Applying skills to content takes more time than acquiring content knowledge. Too many curriculum maps and pacing guides just do not allow teachers the time to provide students opportunities to justify, explain, model, persevere, and connect.

Activities that favor memorization and content acquisition have dominated in too many classrooms because modeling and teaching skills, and providing opportunities for students to practice applying skills, is challenging. Educators are in significant need of professional learning opportunities that focus on students' applying skills to content. And leaders should encourage collaborative teams to focus on how to best guide students in developing these skills within their PLC work.

I do not mean to suggest that content knowledge acquisition is unnecessary in the post-internet age. I'm only suggesting that modeling and teaching skills, and providing students with opportunities to use skills, are essential elements of classroom instruction.

The good news is that modern expert guidance and policy documents agree.

Research-Based Best Practices in Education

While historical curricula, standards, and policies lent themselves to a content-heavy focus, the policy documents, frameworks, and standards in place *since* 2010 are qualitatively distinct—and this is a very good thing. Modern standards increasingly emphasize skills and encourage that these be taught and learned. The newer generation of high-stakes tests *does* require students to apply, reason, and demonstrate deep understanding. This shift is necessary in order to promote equity and design and implement a guaranteed and viable curriculum (see Marzano et al., 2001; Reeves, 2014; Schmoker, 2014), and it better aligns to the world in which we live and for which we are preparing students.

Pre-2010 guidance led teachers to cover content, racing through textbooks in an impossible and misguided effort to get to everything; favor memorization and lower levels of learning; teach procedures, steps, algorithms, and shortcuts; and assess in a surface-level manner using (only) selected-response items. But we know now, more than ever, what to do, and favoring depth over breadth, mastery over coverage, and learning over teaching will better prepare students for the next grade level, and for college, career, and life. Consider the following post-2010 reports and research.

- **The Partnership for 21st Century Learning's** (2019) research on essential future-ready skills has led it to advocate that teachers guide students to practice and master these ten categories of skills.
    - Creativity and innovation
    - Critical thinking and problem solving
    - Communication and collaboration
    - Information and media literacy
    - Technological literacy
    - Flexibility and adaptability
    - Initiative and self-direction
    - Social and cross-cultural skills
    - Productivity and accountability
    - Leadership and responsibility

  These skills are content- and grade-level-agnostic.

- **David Conley's** (2014) research led him to develop a framework for college and career readiness, defined within four categories.
    a. *Think*—Students process information, manipulate it, assemble it, reassemble it, examine it, question it, look for patterns, organize the information, and present it.
    b. *Know*—Students possess foundational knowledge in core subjects.
    c. *Act*—Students employ skills and strategies that enable them to exercise agency and ownership as they manage learning.
    d. *Go*—Students develop skills to navigate college and career challenges.

    Only one category, *know*, relates to academic knowledge. The other categories define skills: self-regulatory, metacognitive, and executive functioning.

- **The Economist Group and Google** have surveyed business leaders to assess the employee attributes that 21st century workplaces most need (Tabary, 2015).
    - Problem solving
    - Teamwork
    - Communication
    - Critical thinking
    - Creativity
    - Leadership
    - Literacy
    - Digital literacy
    - Foreign language ability
    - Emotional intelligence

    The survey reports skills, and the application of knowledge, to be more critical than academics.

- **The Hamilton Project and the Brookings Institution** (Schanzenbach, Nunn, Bauer, Mumford, & Breitwieser, 2016) have analyzed data from the National Longitudinal Survey of Youth, the Armed Forces Qualification Test, the Rotter locus of control scale, the Rosenberg self-esteem scale, and Deming's social skills index. Each of these data sources provides longitudinal data on students, meaning that the impact student characteristics such as self-esteem have on future success can be studied. This research draws the following conclusions.

- The U.S. economy is demanding more noncognitive skills.
- Cognitive and noncognitive skills have strong labor-market payoffs.
- The labor market increasingly rewards noncognitive skills.
- Individuals in the bottom quartile of noncognitive skills are one-third as likely to complete a postsecondary degree as those in the top.
- Noncognitive skill development improves achievement and reduces misbehaviors.
- Preschool interventions emphasizing cognitive and noncognitive skill development have long-term economic benefits.
- A teacher's ability to improve noncognitive skills affects graduation rates more than an ability to raise test scores.

The conclusions are clear. Skills are as important as content; skills may be more important than content. Skills are not yet, however, sufficiently present within academic curricula.

Policy and research encourage skills. But what about new curricular frameworks?

- **Common Core (or next-generation) mathematics** (NGA & CCSSO, 2010b) isn't just composed of content standards with new mathematics standards. Skills such as thinking, explaining, justifying, and applying play an integral part in teaching, learning, and assessing. These skills are represented by the Standards for Mathematical Practice (NGA & CCSSO, 2010b), which state that students should know how to do the following.
    - Make sense of problems and persevere.
    - Reason abstractly and quantitatively.
    - Construct arguments and critique others.
    - Model.
    - Use tools.
    - Attend to precision.
    - Make use of structure.
    - Express regularity in repeated reasoning.

  These skills apply within all domains of mathematics, at all grade levels.

- **Common Core (or next-generation) English language arts** (ELA; NGA & CCSSO, 2010a) features the same increased focus on skills as Common Core mathematics. Students must be able to do the following.
    - Analyze complex texts with evidence.
    - Produce clear and coherent writing appropriate to task, audience, and purpose.
    - Construct arguments and critique others.
    - Build and present knowledge by integrating, comparing, and synthesizing ideas.
    - Build on ideas and articulate clearly when collaborating.
    - Communicate context-specific messages.
    - Use technology and digital media.

    Knowledge isn't enough; students must go deeper—they must *use* their knowledge. And note the similarities of skills between mathematics and English language arts. Again, skills are content agnostic.

- **The Next Generation Science Standards** (NGSS Lead States, 2013) are similarly multidimensional. In fact, the new science standards may make the most progressive leap toward skills, with *crosscutting concepts* and *science and engineering practices* (the skills) complementing *disciplinary core ideas* (the content). The science and engineering practices are as follows.
    - Ask questions and define problems.
    - Develop and use models.
    - Plan and carry out investigations.
    - Analyze and interpret data.
    - Use mathematics.
    - Construct explanations and design solutions.
    - Argue with evidence.
    - Obtain, evaluate, and communicate information.

    Educators are increasingly recognizing and responding to the fact that content is widely accessible; beyond acquiring science knowledge, new standards require students to think and act like scientists—to employ the skills of a scientist.

- **The College, Career, and Civic Life (C3) Framework for Social Studies State Standards** (National Council for the Social Studies, 2013), the newest of the curriculum guides, similarly and explicitly emphasizes skills. Consider the following dimensions of the new social studies framework.
    - Developing questions and planning inquiries
    - Applying concepts from civics, economics, geography, and history
    - Evaluating sources and using evidence
    - Communicating conclusions and taking informed action

    These four dimensions are about *using* disciplinary concepts—about applying the skills of a historian or social scientist.

This focus on skills certainly isn't new. Consider California's historical and social sciences analysis skills categories from 1998 (California Department of Education, 1998).

- Chronological and spatial thinking
- Historical research, evidence, and point of view
- Historical interpretation

These skills can apply to any and all history and social science content, and they can apply in multiple other subject areas. Although a focus on skills that can and should be applied across content areas isn't new, I believe (and am grateful) that schools and educators have made a renewed commitment to genuinely teaching and assessing them.

Many times, perhaps most of the time, common-sense ideas have been around for quite a while. The work in which Irvine Unified School District is engaged, described in the next section of this chapter, finds its origins in Bloom and Webb. Benjamin Bloom developed his taxonomy of educational objectives in 1956. The taxonomy promotes higher forms of thinking, reaching beyond knowledge to comprehension, application, analysis, synthesis, and evaluation. Bloom's taxonomy revised (Anderson, Krathwohl, & Bloom, 2001) reiterates this necessity, substituting verbs for nouns—encouraging students to understand, apply, analyze, and evaluate concepts, processes, procedures, and principles, as well as create (or model) representations of learning, rather than just remember facts. Figure 7.1 (page 116) features Bloom's taxonomy revised.

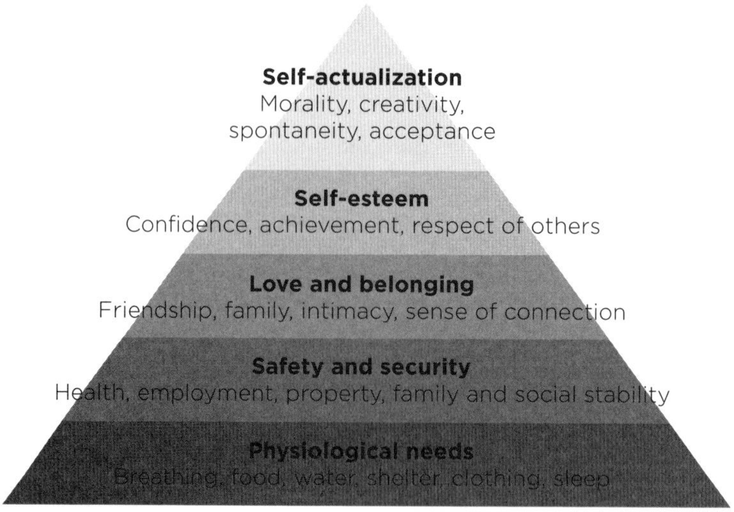

Self-actualization
Morality, creativity, spontaneity, acceptance

Self-esteem
Confidence, achievement, respect of others

Love and belonging
Friendship, family, intimacy, sense of connection

Safety and security
Health, employment, property, family and social stability

Physiological needs
Breathing, food, water, shelter, clothing, sleep

Source: Adapted from Anderson et al., 2001.

Figure 7.1: Bloom's taxonomy revised.

We can most appropriately use Norman Webb's (1997) Depth of Knowledge model to guide and interpret assessment design. Educators have also used this key tool to analyze the cognitive demand and complexity that standards and tasks intend. The model categorizes tasks by the different levels of cognitive demand required to complete them. Level 1 tasks include recall and reproduction, Level 2 tasks include skills and concepts, Level 3 tasks include strategic thinking and reasoning, and Level 4 tasks include extended thinking. Bloom and Webb have both identified that mere knowledge and reproduction are lower-level elements in the education and assessment process. We must guide students in doing more.

An overwhelming amount of research and, more recently, policy supports the fact that skills are as critical as content. And it's common sense. Knowledge isn't worth much if we can't use it. And we won't retain knowledge if we don't use it.

Strategies and Insights for Improving Student Learning

We know what to do, as several policies now make the point that skills are as important as, or more important than, content. We must now apply this knowledge with more frequency, consistency, and success, instead of falling back on historical, memorization-based methods.

This section details several practices that the incredible educators with whom I work have put in place to apply this knowledge. It will discuss:

- Redesigning curricula to emphasize depth over breadth
- Prioritizing skills learning
- Using the claims-evidence-reasoning model
- Evolving homework practices
- Modeling understanding
- Emphasizing inquiry

Redesigning Curricula to Emphasize Depth Over Breadth

From kindergarten to twelfth grade, from science to visual and performing arts, Irvine Unified School District is revisiting and redesigning content areas and courses to favor depth over breadth. That way, knowledge retention improves, learners have time to learn more actively and feel more empowered, and students have time and opportunities to apply skills (Marzano et al., 2001; Popham, 2018; Reeves, 2014; Schmoker, 2014).

Jon Resendez is the social studies department chair at Portola High School in Irvine Unified School District. He also serves as one of the school's educational technology mentors and PLC coaches. Resendez believes that skills learning and an emphasis on depth of curriculum lead to what he refers to as the *significance* of learning:

> It is difficult to memorize anything without constructing personal meaning and endeavoring to apply it. Long-term retention of knowledge comes from the combination of memorization, application, and relevance to the learner. Application plus relevance is what I call *significance*. Students who attempt to only memorize facts will not end up memorizing much at all. This degradation of knowledge has profound implications for the individual and society. (J. Resendez, personal communication, November 13, 2018)

Prioritizing content to favor depth over breadth allows us to better balance knowledge and skills, and balance allows us to meet our mission—which, ultimately, is preparing students for success in college, career, and life. According to Jon Resendez (personal communication, November 13, 2018):

> The primary benefit of a knowledge and skill balance, besides long-term retention, is the ability for students to apply their knowledge to do good in the world. Ultimately, our job as educators is to prepare our learners for anything that might come their way. In order to do that, learners must develop the habit of bridging the gap between knowledge and practice. If students leave us without knowing how to do this, we render the enterprise of education feckless as it pertains to preparing our students for the world.

A creative and engaged citizen never encounters problems where knowledge and skills are disconnected, so why would we separate them in the classroom? The only knowledge assessments that I have encountered in my life are on *Jeopardy!* and at trivia nights.

Prioritizing Skills Learning

Irvine Unified School District secondary science teachers recognize that when prioritizing outcomes, the science and engineering practices (the skills) are critical, and the disciplinary core ideas (the content) are the contexts within which students apply the skills (NGSS Lead States, 2013). We may not need to cover all the content as if it were equally important; it is essential that students learn and have opportunities to apply the skills. Mickey Dickson is the science department chair at Northwood High School in Irvine Unified School District. His courses represent a balance of skills and content knowledge because, as he says:

> Simply put, the consequences (of a lack of balance) are that no learning takes place. By not giving students the opportunity to make connections to their prior knowledge (asking them to model what they think and then testing their model with new information), we do them a grave disservice. It is the process that is more important than the content. (M. Dickson, personal communication, December 4, 2018)

In his lessons, students learn content *through* the skills acquisition process. He notes:

> Over the past few years I have leaned more and more on inquiry-based instruction, almost to the exclusion of any direct instruction. We can provide information to students by means of inquiry. Process-Oriented Guided Inquiry Learning (POGIL) is a great example. Students work with the new material by interpreting models and creating inferences to answer questions. The answers they generate are then "put to the test" with additional models. Oftentimes, they will need to go back to the original models and reinterpret. At any rate, they are acquiring content via application. These two should not be separate ideas. They are intertwined. In the end, as I tell my students, you may or may not remember the specific content years from now, but you will remember how to struggle, self-assess, and modify your understanding. (M. Dickson, personal communication, December 4, 2018)

Applying knowledge and skills gained during initial instruction at different times to different tasks, often and before an assessment, is common sense that is common in Mickey's classroom but not common enough in others. The National Research Council definitively reported on this conclusion in 2000. While significant time will need to be devoted to lessons during which students are asked to apply learning, the process is simple: in the days following the introduction and initial practice of a concept, assign tasks in which students practice new skills and apply newly acquired knowledge to a unique task, one that is similar to the original tasks but distinct enough that students will likely need to reflect several sets of skills and knowledge to which they have been exposed and select the right approach. Importantly, students can practice the behavioral skills described in chapter 5 (for example, mindsets and perseverance) during these applications. By prioritizing essential standards (as described in detail within chapter 1) and intentionally planning time for application, learning will improve.

Using the Claims-Evidence-Reasoning Model

Teachers in Irvine Unified School District have adopted the claims-evidence-reasoning (CER) model. Using this model, the teachers require students from kindergarten to high school, in all content areas, to make and justify claims with evidence. In grade 6 and above, teachers additionally ask students to add reasoning to their claim and evidence—to provide a reasoned explanation that connects the claim they have made and the evidence they have given. The CER model is a central, commonsense strategy that reinforces skills and guides teachers and students in applying skills to content knowledge.

Evolving Homework Practices

A common lament among educators is that students do not remember content from a few months before, and consequently, they are not successful on tasks that require this prior learning. Another common concern from educators and families is that students are not always successful when completing homework that asks them to practice tasks using knowledge and skills taught earlier that day, in the event that this new knowledge and these new skills were not learned completely or correctly.

Two simple strategies, ones used by an increasing number of educators in Irvine Unified School District, are *lagging homework* and *spiral reviews*. In lagging homework, the evening's assignment asks students to practice tasks that use knowledge and skills learned days and even a few weeks before. Spiral reviews are additions to transitional homework assignments that ask students to practice that day's learning; teachers add a few tasks to the homework assignment that require students to re-engage with content and skills learned earlier in the year. The goal is to increase retention and to ensure that, when presented with new situations, students can successfully access and apply previously learned skills.

Modeling Understanding

Irvine Unified School District teachers ask students to model their understanding and explain why their models make sense. Students have various ways of modeling their understanding. Models can include schematics, diagrams, visual representations, and concrete objects, and they also could be metaphors and formulas. Additionally, teachers are much more regularly requiring students to explain and justify approaches and solutions. These skills of modeling, explaining, and justifying are critical in all content areas.

Emphasizing Inquiry

Irvine Unified School District's teachers of AP courses are eagerly following the College Board's (2018) redesigns, which will result in a greater emphasis on inquiry, reasoning, and communication skills and a better balance between breadth and depth. As we strive to increase equity and access, we are working to ensure that the sheer quantity of content to cover in advanced courses does not compromise *some* students' success and limit *all* students' future success in specific disciplines.

Since the shift toward common standards (initially at the state level) prompted by *A Nation at Risk* (National Commission on Excellence in Education, 1983), this more recent shift toward applying skills to content, as opposed to simply acquiring content knowledge, may represent the most significant curricular change we've experienced in several decades.

Conclusion

We all must commit to thinking and doing differently in our teaching within content areas and courses so that we prepare our students for the realities and demands of 21st century society and workplaces. Knowledge and skills have an inextricable link. Careers that lead to a living wage and a successful adult life increasingly require that individuals are adaptive to situations that they encounter in the workplace (Schanzenbach et al., 2016). Jon Resendez (personal communication, November 13, 2018) says it very well:

> In the discipline of social studies and beyond, we need to stop seeing knowledge and skills as mutually exclusive ideas. Students must seek knowledge in the context of doing something with it. Collaborative activity should be the norm, and individual work should be the exception. In an ideal situation, students would transcend the mere dissemination of knowledge to others by simulating public institutions like legislatures and courts, arguing policy perspectives, and engaging in service projects. This means that there is no such thing as a "knowledge assessment" or

a "skills assessment"; they are one and the same. Our students may not remember every single standard out there; no student can. But if skills and knowledge serve each other, then students will gain a deep understanding of the standards that are most relevant to their lives and the ability to make the world better through their education.

If we want students to apply what they learn in grades K–12 when they enter college or a skilled career, it's common sense that we must model and teach reasoning skills and provide opportunities to apply and employ these skills. It's common sense that we should have a better balance of content and skills. In the next chapter, I'll describe common-sense ways that we can engage students with rigorous learning experiences, through which they can apply rich skills.

Next Steps

Please complete the following next steps as you consider changes that may be appropriate for your school or district to ensure that you value skills as much as or more than content.

1. Examine current practices by considering the following questions.
   - How much class time is spent on knowledge building and acquisition, and how much class time is spent on applying, explaining, justifying, and reasoning with content knowledge?
   - To what extent do learning targets and class and course outcomes balance content acquisition and skill application?
   - To what extent are Bloom's levels 4–6 and Webb's levels 3–4 part of the rich learning experiences with which students engage?
   - To what extent do assessments and other evidence-gathering tools match the higher-level-thinking skills that students are increasingly asked to perform?
   - In what ways might pacing guides or curriculum maps unintentionally, through rigidities, limit the amount of time that students spend engaged in deeper thinking?
   - In what ways does the quantity of content within guides and maps inhibit teachers' ability to engage students in deeper thinking?
   - How have professional learning opportunities built educators' capacity to embed skills practice with content acquisition?
   - How has the work of PLCs enhanced teams' capacity to embed skills practice with content acquisition?
   - How do leaders encourage and reinforce the need to embed skills practice with content acquisition?

2. Discover research- and evidence-based common-sense practices by doing the following.
   - Re-explore the frameworks and standards for your subject area, or the content within your grade level, and make sense of the shifts within these documents that emphasize the skills that students must develop.
   - Dedicate class time within periods, days, units, and years to knowledge acquisition and skill application for new concepts, content, and skills that have been introduced and initially practiced.
   - Ensure that collaborative teams consider behavioral (or *soft* or *noncognitive*) skills (see chapter 5, page 73) and embed these

within learning experiences along with the skills represented in Bloom's (1956) taxonomy, Webb's (1997) Depth of Knowledge model, the Standards for Mathematical Practice (NGA & CCSSO, 2010b), and the science and engineering practices of the Next Generation Science Standards (NGSS Lead States, 2013).

- Reflect on pedagogies, lesson designs, and strategies that you use in class, and learn about and implement practices that extend student learning beyond knowledge acquisition.
- Revisit pacing guides and curriculum maps to ensure that you have time to differentiate teaching and learning and give students opportunities to apply, explain, justify, and reason.
- Consider making processing activities like claims-evidence-reasoning a staple of students' processing of knowledge and information in all content areas.
- Ensure that assessments are measuring students' ability to apply reasoning skills, and use evidence generated through these assessments to inform future teaching and learning.

3. Identify what you will stop doing, and develop a stop-doing plan.
4. Identify what you will start doing, and develop a start-doing plan.

8
Promoting Rigorous Learning Tasks

Designing a guaranteed and viable curriculum, one that allows teachers and students to focus on depth and avoid the consequences of breadth, is not enough. Engaging students in their learning through active learning strategies, so that students do more of the thinking, talking, and doing, is not enough. And ensuring that curriculum represents a balance of content, concepts, and skills, so that students can apply and make sense of the content knowledge they acquire, is not enough.

It's common sense that we must also ensure that students engage with rigorous tasks. Understanding what rigor is and isn't, and providing rigorous learning experiences for all students, will deepen learning, help make learning relevant, and better prepare students for college, skilled careers, and life. To illustrate the importance of this chapter's common-sense leadership practice, the following sections will detail educational practices that defy common sense, research-based best practices in education, and strategies and insights for improving student learning.

Educational Practices That Defy Common Sense

We could not do our work as educators without curricular resources, and textbooks have historically been our most common resource. Unfortunately, many textbooks contain mostly low-level, rote, and one-step tasks. Even when textbooks promise to have more rigorous tasks (often at the end of the lesson), they are, in fact, simplistic problems in disguise, or educators do not assign the rigorous tasks.

Educators also commonly use worksheets as their curricular resources. But as professional development expert Marcia Tate (2016) notes, worksheets don't grow dendrites—in other words, the completion of low-level tasks typically represented within worksheets does not ask students to complete tasks of richness and rigor. Relying on worksheets has detrimental effects because too many worksheets require students to just fill in blanks and solve procedural problems. And far too often, we believe that assigning more problems, or longer readings, or longer writing assignments, or problems with bigger numbers increases rigor. We believe that we are increasing rigor by requiring more.

In the previous chapter (page 109), I noted that some educators continue to focus on content over skills because they planned backward from earlier generations of high-stakes assessments, which favored lower levels of understanding. The same situation has occurred in respect to the quality of tasks. While the quality of high-stakes assessments has shifted, too many educator-created or textbook-provided assessments continue to focus on simplistic tasks. When teachers plan backward from assessments like these, tasks too often lack rigor.

Facilitating rigorous tasks will take more time, and having students complete rigorous tasks will undoubtedly involve productive struggle and healthy frustration. As long as mindsets remain fixed, and as long as students and teachers alike equate learning with points, percentages, and grades (Schimmer, 2016), students, educators, and parents will be reluctant to engage in more rigorous learning. (Please see chapter 5, page 73, and *Behavior: The Forgotten Curriculum* [Weber, 2018] for more information on addressing fixed mindsets.)

We must increase the quality of the tasks with which we ask students to engage. We have several common-sense ways of doing this.

Research-Based Best Practices in Education

On the topic of rigor, we have a wealth of best practices and guidance on which to draw. To start, the seven principles that compose the instructional core, which chapter 1 of Elizabeth City, Richard Elmore, Sarah Fiarman, and Lee Teitel's (2009) *Instructional Rounds in Education* describes, are among the most important ideals that ought to guide our work. Principle 4 is "The task predicts performance":

> What determines what students know and are able to do is not what the curriculum says they are supposed to do, nor even what the teacher thinks he or she is asking students to do. What predicts performance is

what students are actually doing. Memorization tasks produce fluency in memorization and recall, not necessarily understanding. Memorizing the elements of the periodic table is not the same as understanding the properties of the elements. The single biggest observational discipline we have to teach people in our networks is to look on top of the students' desk, rather than at the teacher in front of the room. The only way to find out what students are actually doing is to observe what they are doing—not, unfortunately, to ask teachers what students have done after the fact, and even less to look at the results of student work after they have engaged in the task. (City et al., 2009, p. 30)

If we want student learning to improve, then the nature of the tasks that we assign to students must improve.

Barbara Blackburn (2014), author of *Rigor in Your Classroom*, defines both what rigor isn't and what it is (see table 8.1). She states that rigorous, complex tasks are for all students, and these tasks involve *multiple* contexts, sources, steps, and perspectives.

Table 8.1: What Rigor Isn't and Is

What Rigor Isn't	What Rigor Is
• Lots of homework • Additional items to solve • Only for some • Only possible if scaffolds and supports are provided • Only possible with the right resources	• Transferring understanding to new contexts • Synthesizing multiple sources • Employing multiple complex steps • Approaching tasks from divergent perspectives

Source: Adapted from Blackburn, 2014.

Sandra Kaplan and colleagues created categories of depth and complexity to represent rigor (Kaplan, Gould, & Siegel, 1995). These categories of depth are:

- Using the language of the discipline
- Discovering the big idea
- Determining the essential details
- Identifying rules, patterns, and trends
- Proposing unanswered questions
- Investigating ethics

The icons of complexity are:

- Describing change over time
- Approaching solutions from multiple points of view
- Making connections across the disciplines

Tasks that align with Kaplan's icons ask students to go deeper and think more complexly; they make a task more rigorous.

Finally, Art Costa and Bena Kallick (2000) present habits of mind that will be present in rigorous tasks, and that teachers can infuse into student experiences in order to increase their rigor. Costa and Kallick (2000) find that rigorous tasks require students to:

- Persist and manage impulsivity
- Communicate with clarity, accuracy, and precision
- Gather data through all senses
- Listen with empathy
- Create, imagine, and innovate
- Think flexibly and interdependently
- Respond with wonderment and awe
- Think about thinking
- Take intellectual risks
- Find humor
- Question and pose problems
- Apply past knowledge to new situations
- Remain open to continuous learning

Like Kaplan et al. (1995), Costa and Kallick (2000) note that rigor does not mean asking students to do *more* work; rigor requires students to *do more with* the work.

The following section will detail ways in which educators and educator leaders can follow this research's advice and promote rigorous learning tasks to improve student learning. It will also provide helpful advice from leaders in the field to guide leaders on their journeys.

Strategies and Insights for Improving Student Learning

Readers may notice the inextricable link between this chapter's and the previous chapter's topics. It will be difficult, if not impossible, to increase the rigor of a task without requiring students to learn and apply skills within the task. In chapter 7 (page 109), I described how we should strive to ensure that tasks balance skills *and* content. In the remainder of this chapter, I'll share the common-sense approaches that Irvine Unified School District is taking to (1) create a learning environment that invites and supports students to do rigorous tasks, and (2) increase the rigor of what students do within tasks.

Creating a Rigor-Friendly Learning Environment

Moving toward more rigorous tasks requires schools to first set up a learning environment that supports both teachers and students when faced with rigor. A rigor-friendly environment would have students seated in groups in which they can collaborate with rich tasks. Work stations (perhaps simply a few tables in a corner of the room) would be available for students from the same or different table groups to work together. And, there would be easy access to tools and technologies that would facilitate and provide resources for students to successfully engage with rigorous tasks.

Maureen Leong is one of Irvine Unified School District's exceptional secondary mathematics teachers. A three-decade teaching veteran, she recently returned to the classroom after an incredibly influential stint as a teacher on special assignment at the district office. Leong believes strongly in the concept of rigor, noting that students whom teachers do not challenge are at risk of becoming disengaged. She states, "Many times the students are bored because the work they're assigned looks just like what they've done previously. They don't understand why they're 'learning' the material. Many times these students become our behavior issues" (M. Leong, personal communication, November 15, 2018). She believes that rigor contributes to relevance:

> I think that students have more of a buy-in with rigorous tasks. They see the relevance of why they're doing the math. I like the fact that by doing a variety of tasks, different students can excel when they might struggle at other times; this can definitely build their self-confidence. (M. Leong, personal communication, November 15, 2018)

Leong's classroom is an excellent example of a positive learning environment that invites rigorous learning. She has created an intellectually safe environment that provides a foundation for rigor, stating, "Students definitely need to be in an environment in which they feel comfortable to take risks and make mistakes. If they do, they are more open to thinking of new ideas and trying things out" (M. Leong, personal communication, November 15, 2018). A visitor to her classroom will see the students working collaboratively on the whiteboards that cover every classroom wall. She teaches and students learn by representing mathematics in multiple forms—concretely, pictorially, and abstractly. The physical layout of Maureen's classroom, and the way that she expertly utilizes this space, provide nearly constant opportunities for students to engage in rigorous tasks.

We in Irvine Unified School District respect that engaging students in rigorous tasks may represent a shift, and we rely on collaborative teams to successfully make these shifts. According to Maureen Leong (personal communication, November 15, 2018):

> I feel the best way to implement more rigorous tasks is through collaboration. Teachers need to be open to share what they're trying—what worked and what didn't and what can maybe be tweaked to work better. I've found fun and engaging activities through Twitter, using hashtags like #MTBOS [Math Twitter Blog-o-Sphere]. Three-Act Tasks, as well as Open Middle and Illustrative Mathematics problems, have given my students the opportunity to work at their level. What's rigorous for some students is quite different than what is rigorous to another.

Further, prioritizing key learning outcomes can also help teachers prime a classroom for rigor. Prioritizing key learning outcomes, already discussed in depth within this book, allows teachers and students the time to get to greater levels of depth. This creates space within lessons, units, and the school to get to greater levels of rigor. As described in chapter 1 (page 15), a primary reason to embrace "teach less, learn more" is so that the depth and rigor of learning can increase.

Once they've primed the learning environment for exploration and rigor, teachers can begin increasing the rigor of the tasks themselves.

Increasing the Rigor of Tasks

The following are a few specific examples of how the incredible educators in Irvine Unified School District are increasing the rigor of tasks.

Within classrooms and innovation labs, students are engaging in project-based learning (PBL) and PBL-like tasks. Students generate key questions, choose the challenge to address their questions, develop their plan for dealing with the challenge, identify and use the resources they need, and prepare a solution that they share with an audience, even when the audience is their peers. Teachers guide students to select rigorous projects that require depth within the investigation and the solution.

We are committed to developing, administering, and collectively analyzing *common formative assessments* of greater rigor that will inform future teaching and learning. These assessments include tasks that are open-ended instead of selected-response, tasks that require students to explain and justify, and tasks that ask students to apply learning to unique situations—in other words, tasks that are more rigorous. We are also collectively designing and engaging students in *common learning experiences*. These learning experiences are longer than a lesson but shorter than a unit. Within the common learning experience, students explore a topic, develop explanations, apply learning to new contexts, and conclude by creating a product that represents the growth in their learning. Our goal is that rigorous tasks like common learning experiences allow and require students to struggle, and make it safe for them to engage in intellectual risk taking.

Inspired by Susan Looney's Same but Different Math (www.samebutdifferentmath.com) and the research-based power of comparing and contrasting (Marzano, 2003), our teachers are designing tasks in a same-but-different format. This format presents students in kindergarten through grade 12 with two similar problems or situations. They then have to identify what's the same and what's different as part of their problem solving. Like Maureen Leong, Kristie Donavan is a former exceptional and influential teacher on special assignment who is back in the classroom as an exceptional and influential teacher at Woodbridge High School in Irvine Unified School District. She regularly uses same-but-different tasks and intentionally strives to infuse rigor into teaching and learning. Donavan states:

> When we give students tasks that lack rigor, we send a message to students that they are not worthy or capable of challenging mathematics. And yet, a lot of teachers (and students and parents, for that matter) think rigor equals "hard." A rigorous task should be challenging, yet accessible. It should have multiple entry points. A student should be able to choose his or her own path through a problem and explain his or her thinking. A rigorous task should make students' brains sweat—and students should feel like all of that sweat was for a purpose!
>
> In addition to improving the quality of our tasks, we need to allow ourselves time for rigorous tasks in class. I always feel like I've done my best teaching when I do one great problem, not twenty mediocre problems. It is so important to allow time for students to share their thinking, compare methods, make connections between representations, and make connections to prior knowledge, and we don't do it

often enough when we're worried about cramming in all of the standards. (K. Donavan, personal communication, November 6, 2018)

When students get through a lot of problems or get through a problem quickly, that is a pretty good (and common-sense) indicator that rigor is absent.

Developed by Mary Bourassa (2019), *Which One Doesn't Belong?* is a similar way of presenting and organizing tasks for students. It presents students with four images, equations, or short sections of text, each in its own quadrant, and asks them to choose which of the four does not belong and justify why the selection does not belong. The genius of Which One Doesn't Belong? is that students could justify each of the four quadrants as not belonging. Tasks like this have a low floor and a high ceiling, a quality we strive for all tasks to possess so that all students can access the learning and the tasks stretch all students. Which One Doesn't Belong? tasks have a low floor because one of the four options is typically relatively straightforward in its differentness, although a justification is of course necessary. And these tasks have a high ceiling because teachers can challenge students to generate another justification for their selection or to develop justifications for the other three quadrants.

Our teachers are designing open-ended tasks, meaning that the tasks have multiple entry points, multiple approaches, multiple solutions, and multiple ways of representing solutions. Sometimes, however, multiple solutions are simply not an option. In these cases, we strive to make sure that tasks have an *open middle*, a term coined by Robert Kaplinsky, Nanette Johnson, Bryan Anderson, Dan Luevanos, and Zack Miller (www.openmiddle.com). The term *open middle* refers to the design of the tasks; students will begin and end in the same place but what they do in the middle—how they get to the solution—may be different.

We follow the work of Jo Boaler (2018), who describes the importance of combining positive mindsets with multiplicity. We interpret *multiplicity* as a synonym for, and a way of articulating, rigor. Boaler (2018) describes multiplicity as students' making connections between concepts within and between disciplines *and* thinking flexibly by using multiple approaches and representations. She further suggests that if students finish assignments quickly as we inspire them to reach for rigor, it may actually reveal that students have not committed to depth and rigor. We may need to have patience with our students, including students for whom learning comes relatively easily, when we introduce more rigorous tasks. We have perhaps unintentionally conditioned students to expect tasks that involve lower-level thinking, that are completed relatively quickly, and do not require some struggle. A positive mindset, and perseverance, will be required when engaging with more rigorous assignments.

She also reports that high-achieving students don't necessarily possess more content knowledge than other students; they simply employ more flexible thinking. We are incorporating the principles of multiplicity and positive mindsets into the tasks that we design so that students are regularly engaging, interacting, and solving tasks of increased rigor.

Educators must examine the quantity of what we teach, the way in which we teach, and what students are doing within the learning process. We must also examine the quality of the work within which and from which students learn, so that the rigor of tasks matches the expectations we have for achieving mastery of the standards and the realities that they will face in their futures.

Conclusion

It's common sense: "What predicts performance is *what students are actually doing*" (City et al., 2009, p. 30). The requirements of 21st century society and workplaces—and student success in college and skilled careers—demand that we design and deliver more rigorous tasks. As a first step, we must determine what rigor isn't and is. Then, as chapter 1 (page 15) described, we must ensure that we create a guaranteed and viable curriculum that allows students the space to engage in rigorous tasks, which require and deserve more time than low-level tasks. The examples provided in the previous section of this chapter represent how we in Irvine Unified School District are beginning to bring all students to rigor.

The common-sense ideas that this book has described thus far relate to what occurs *within* schools. But there is a potentially powerful resource outside school buildings that we have not yet fully realized—*parents*. This idea is also common sense—parents will become the partners we need them to be and they want to be when we empower them. The next chapter will describe the power of parent partnerships.

Next Steps

Please complete the following next steps as you consider changes that may be appropriate for your school or district so you can help students learn more by increasing the rigor of tasks.

1. Examine current practices by considering the following questions.
   - To what extent do teachers assign low-level, rote, and one-step tasks?
   - To what extent do teachers assign truly rigorous word problems? If you remove the contexts, how many of these problems are, in fact, procedural tasks?
   - How do you define *rigor*? How often do teachers (incorrectly) attempt to increase rigor by assigning more problems, or longer readings, or longer writing assignments, or problems with bigger numbers?
   - In what ways might pacing guides or curriculum maps unintentionally direct teachers and students to engage in tasks of lower rigor levels?
   - In what ways does the quantity of content in curriculum guides and maps inhibit teachers' ability to assign and facilitate the completion of more rigorous tasks?
   - How have professional learning opportunities built educators' capacity to curate or create rigorous tasks?
   - How has the work of PLCs enhanced teams' capacities to collaboratively curate or create rigorous tasks and learn from student performance on these tasks so they can support students to greater levels of success?
   - To what extent does the completion of worksheets or low-level sets of problems represent the depth and sequence of learning in classrooms? For example, do students receive a different sheet or set each day with numerous problems, or are students asked to complete fewer problems that require multiple steps, more complex investigation, or explanations and justifications?
   - How are leaders encouraging and reinforcing the need for more rigorous tasks?

2. Discover research- and evidence-based common-sense practices by doing the following.
   - Ask students to transfer their understanding from current tasks to new contexts.

- Assign tasks that require students to access, synthesize, and apply information from multiple sources.
- Ensure that several items within tasks require students to complete multiple steps.
- Ask students to solve current tasks by approaching the questions or problems from different perspectives.
- Ensure that students successfully complete assigned problems and tasks.
- Create, curate, and assign tasks that are relevant to students or, in terms of the Next Generation Science Standards (NGSS Lead States, 2013), tasks that are relevant to students' lives.
- Design tasks that require more than one session to complete.
- Explore Kaplan's depth and complexity icons (page 127) and Costa and Kallick's habits of mind (page 128), and consider enhancing current tasks by asking students to choose one icon or habit and apply it to the task.
- Empower students to generate their own questions and create their own tasks.
- Strive to curate or create tasks that have low floors and high ceilings.
- Increasingly assign tasks for which there are multiple approaches or multiple solutions.

3. Identify what you will stop doing, and develop a stop-doing plan.
4. Identify what you will start doing, and develop a start-doing plan.

NGSS Lead States. (2013). Next Generation Science Standards: For states, by states. Washington, DC: National Academies Press.

9

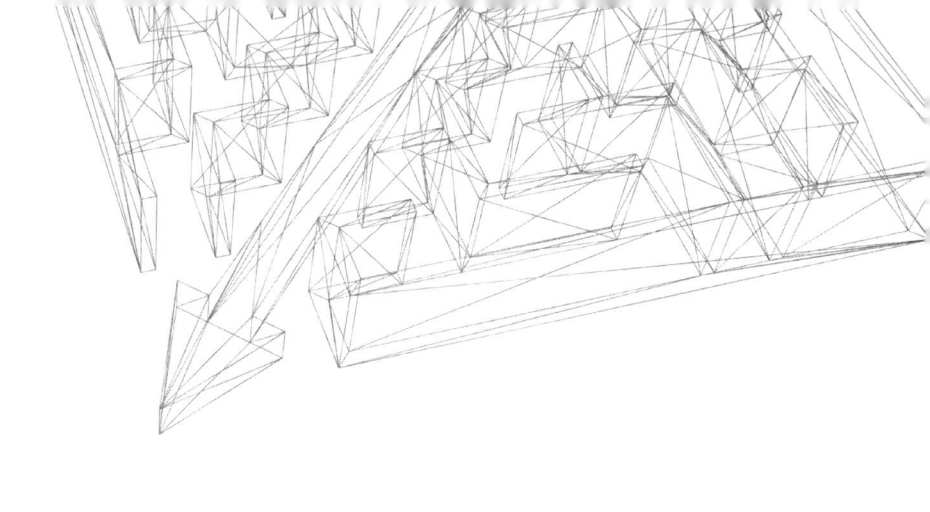

Empowering Parents as Partners in Education

Parental involvement and support from home—or the lack thereof—are consistent topics of conversation at schools across the United States and across the world. Here are a few truths related to this topic that Irvine Unified School District schools have accepted.

- Almost all parents are doing the best they can.
- Almost all parents are doing what they think they should do and what they know to do.
- If we want parents to do differently and do more, we need to take the lead on communicating the important elements of a more powerful partnership.

As is so often the case, *we* are the answer we've been waiting for. It's common sense: parents are potentially powerful and positive partners. Schools and school leaders need to do a better job of inviting and empowering this partnership. To illustrate the importance of this chapter's common-sense leadership practice, the following sections will detail educational practices that defy common sense, research-based best practices in education, and strategies and insights for improving student learning.

Educational Practices That Defy Common Sense

Unfortunately, too often, our interactions about and with parents involve and are limited to the following.

- **Too much telling, not enough listening:** Yes, we have curricular frameworks and standards that we must follow and communicate. And yes, we are the professionals, so we have knowledge to share with parents. Much of the time, we tell parents what to do without listening to their feedback and questions, responding to their needs, or incorporating their suggestions. But as chapter 2 (page 31) described, leaders also listen, and they lead this partnership. I invite all of us educators to more frequently and authentically listen to the hopes, needs, and ideas of parents and the community, and I encourage us to use the products of that learned information to inform what occurs in school and what supports we provide.

- **The shaming in blaming:** Hoping and wringing our hands about what we wish parents would do and what parents should do may be cathartic in the short term, but it is unempowering and unprofessional. I believe that we, both intellectually and emotionally, know that families are in various states of *just getting by*. Empathy demands that we respect, love, honor, and accept our students' families for who they are and where they are. They would do anything for their children. Perhaps we ought to ask ourselves, "What can they do? What do we most want them to do? How have we and can we support them in doing it?" Let's ask these questions with high expectations and a pragmatic respect for reality. There's a pretty good chance that parents don't have a crystal-clear understanding of what they should do. There's also a pretty good chance that we haven't made our communications and requests as clear and comprehensive as they could be.

- **Homework:** Here's a thought—we should never assign a homework assignment unless we have evidence that students can complete it successfully and independently. Supporting students in the successful completion of homework is a task to which all parents are committed and a task with which all schools would appreciate support. But when homework is too long or difficult to understand, or requires parents to provide assistance that they may not have the time or the specific strategies to provide, we put parents in an impossible situation. If we don't check that students will have the time and the skills to complete a homework assignment, our manner of assigning homework seems all but guaranteed to put parents at a disadvantage and on the defensive.

- **Back-to-school nights and open houses:** Both back-to-school nights and open house events are wonderful opportunities to celebrate our schools, students, families, communities, and educators. It occurs to me that we can perhaps rethink their purpose and format. These two events alone, in their current form, are not sufficient to nurture the partnerships that we need and desire. If we want parents to be parents, and if we want them more involved in their children's education, then we need to dedicate time to nurturing these partnerships and to use this time to provide relevant information and specific supports. I have observed schools making significant shifts in these experiences for parents. For example, one elementary school hosted an evening in which parents learned how their children would be taught to add, subtract, multiply, and divide whole numbers by participating in actual minilessons. Parents left with simple activities that they could complete at home that matched the process and expectations of the classroom. A middle school hosted a series of parent evenings that described the statewide testing procedures and reports that would be sent home, as well as what within-district assessments were used for and the information that schools and parents would receive. I challenge us to continue to make these shifts and to increase the quantity and quality of these events and partnerships with parents.

Research-Based Best Practices in Education

Good research and plenty of evidence-based best practices provide guidance on the best ways of partnering with parents and communities.

The seven correlates of effective schools and the effective schools movement (Edmonds, 1979; Lezotte & Snyder, 2010) remain some of the most important and impactful contributions to U.S. public education. The seven correlates represent characteristics of schools that significantly outperform other schools serving similar communities, and several pertain to parent partnerships.

1. **Clear and focused mission:** Parents should and can contribute to creating and promoting this mission.
2. **High expectations for success:** Parents need to know what the high expectations mean. Parents should be provided with the information to answer these questions: With what tasks do students engage? What do students produce? What should students learn?

3. **Strong instructional leadership:** School principals and leaders clearly, consistently, and passionately communicate best practices and the urgency that every student reach high levels of learning to all stakeholders, including parents.

4. **Frequent monitoring of student progress:** Parents deserve to know where their children currently are in their learning journey and where they need to be, beyond a letter grade.

5. **Opportunity to learn or time on task:** Parents can support the necessary shifts in what students are doing and how they're doing it in classrooms when they understand why classrooms may not look the same as when they were in school.

6. **Safe and orderly environment:** Parents should be key contributors to the system of behavioral supports and the behavioral expectations that the school establishes. Schools should ensure that parents do not see the reinforcement of safe, orderly, and productive environments as something that schools *do* to their children; instead, parents should understand guidance given to their children regarding behavioral skills as positively and productively reinforcing and providing feedback on students' development of essential nonacademic, behavioral skills.

7. **Positive school–home relations:** This seventh correlate speaks for itself. Exceptional schools enjoy positive school-home relations.

In *The New Meaning of Educational Change*, Michael Fullan (2016) examines the role of parental involvement in schools:

> Teachers cannot do it alone. Parents and other community members are crucial and largely untapped resources who have (or can be helped to have) assets and expertise that are essential to the partnership . . . parents are their children's very first educators. They have knowledge of their children that is not available to anyone else. They have a vested and committed interest in their children's success, and they also have valuable knowledge and skills to contribute that spring from their interests, hobbies, occupations, and place in the community. (p. 159)

Fullan is suggesting schools in which educators learn from and with parents in their service of students and student learning.

In *Teaching With Poverty in Mind* and *Engaging Students With Poverty in Mind*, Eric Jensen (2009, 2013) summarizes the research, and promotes a model, that says parent education and empowerment are foundational elements of combatting the effects of socioeconomic challenges. He notes researchers have concluded that "many of the factors of low socioeconomic status that negatively affect student academic success could be overcome by better educating parents about these essential needs [emotional challenges, stressors, and physical health]" (Jensen, 2009, p. 39). Significantly involving parents, providing supports to parents and families (in school-based areas and areas beyond school, such as medical care), reaching out to families in their homes, and building strong relationships with parents are highly correlated with improved student outcomes.

Anthony Muhammad (2018) has led buildings, and supported hundreds of other schools, that have achieved remarkable gains in student achievement in part due to parents' foundational contributions. He makes an airtight case for the transformational impacts of parental involvement and suggests that schools might create parent universities (within which parents learn about how schools work), have staff serve as parent liaisons, seek parent volunteers, and actively involve parents in governance.

Last, and perhaps most significantly, the Comer School Development Program (Comer et al., 1996) provides over a half century of research and practice validating a model for school improvement and governance that prioritizes parent and community involvement. The model is built on a common-sense idea described in chapter 5 (page 73): that when children have positive relationships with adults, it directly leads to more positive outcomes. The authors of the Comer report state, "Children need positive interactions with adults in order to develop adequately" (Comer et al., 1996, p. 28). The Comer School Development Program enthusiastically involves parents and community members in the school-improvement process.

Schools in the Comer program have three key teams: (1) the parent team, (2) the school planning and management team, and (3) the student and staff support team. The parent team is, of course, composed of parents and expects that every single parent will have active involvement in some facet of the school. However, parents are actually involved in all three teams; key and unique areas of focus for each team's work include child development, child psychology, and the creation of 360-degree, wraparound supports for students and families from across the school and community. Authentic parental involvement isn't an afterthought or a compliance-oriented activity; parents are very real participants. Recognizing the realities that can limit parental involvement, Comer schools emphasize creating opportunities, through communitywide partnerships, for parents and other community adults (including, of course, educators at the school) to serve as role models for students.

The benefits of the Comer School Development Program include improved social skills, attendance, student learning, self-efficacy, relationships with adults, mental health, achievement on standardized tests, classroom grades, teacher enthusiasm, and of course parental involvement (Comer et al., 1996). This makes sense: in Comer schools, the entire school community systematically and proactively partners for student success, and leadership is widely distributed (as discussed in chapter 10, page 149); this empowerment and sense of belonging improve school-based outcomes (Walton & Cohen, 2007, 2011).

Parental involvement has such potentially positive impacts that we simply cannot leave it to chance:

> Engagement with families should not be viewed as peripheral or tangential to school improvement efforts. There is significant evidence that strong parent engagement practices are related to student achievement. Students who have involved parents are more likely to earn higher grades and test scores, and enroll in higher-level classes; be promoted to the next grade level, pass their classes, and earn more credits; and attend school regularly. Student achievement tends to be higher in schools where principals and teachers are open to parent engagement and view parents as partners in the learning process. Further, there is a substantial body of evidence that parental involvement influences the development of academic mindsets across multiple dimensions. (Allensworth et al., 2018, p. 21)

It's common sense and research based: while parental outreach certainly requires hard work and an enthusiastic commitment from school staff, increased quantities and types of parental involvement lead to better outcomes for communities, schools, and students.

The following section will discuss strategies that educators can use to make parents true partners in their children's education. Words of advice and wisdom from experienced teachers and leaders will supplement these strategies and examples.

Strategies and Insights for Improving Student Learning

Schools and school districts that have made the effort to prioritize outreach have used specific approaches to achieve success with parental involvement. Here are just a few strategies that schools have used to empower parents.

- Implementing the ten educational commandments for parents
- Surveying and responding to parent needs

- Including parents as interventionists
- Making common sense more common

Implementing the Ten Educational Commandments for Parents

The ten educational commandments for parents (2019), created by the Orange County Business Council in partnership with the Latino Educational Attainment Initiative, may be the most remarkable parent empowerment initiative I've ever encountered. The ten educational commandments for parents are as follows:

> Parents will—
> 1. Commit as a family to be involved in school
> 2. Do our part in helping our child study
> 3. Understand how grades work
> 4. Learn how schools are structured
> 5. Learn what our child needs to graduate successfully from high school
> 6. Support the learning of mathematics, science, and English
> 7. Encourage our child to take honors and advanced courses
> 8. Help our child prepare to be college and/or career ready
> 9. Realize college options are affordable
> 10. Teach our child to be creative, to communicate, and to view challenges as opportunities

Guided by parents, for parents, this program doesn't simply expect parents to embrace and practice the commandments; rather, parents learn the why, what, and how that each commandment represents. In combination with educators within schools and districts that embrace and support the commandments, parents are empowered to significantly and actively contribute to their children's educational lives.

Surveying and Responding to Parent Needs

Garden Grove Unified School District's parent partnership has long been a key to the success of this award-winning California district. This district was an early implementer of the ten educational commandments for parents. Now, as part of its comprehensive and cutting-edge commitment to college and career readiness for all, the district extensively surveys parents for their opinions and experiences. These evidence points are as important to all educators in the district as grades and test scores, and they directly shape continuous improvement efforts.

Michelle Pinchot is a principal in Garden Grove Unified School District who has coauthored, with Michael Fullan and others, articles on the topic of school leadership

(Fullan & Pinchot, 2018; Pinchot & Weber, 2016). She is a master of authentically involving parents and has done so at multiple schools. Pinchot says that one of her prior schools developed grade-level parent meetings and held them each trimester:

> Topics were created by both the teachers and the parents. We imitated classroom instruction and had parents experience learning firsthand with their child so that they could better support at home. This was highly successful because it was a shared vision by school and parents. (M. Pinchot, personal communication, November 12, 2018)

At her current school, Heritage Computer Science Academy, Pinchot says:

> Our parents have requested help with immigration, learning English, and understanding how to navigate the U.S. school system. We've started training parents in computer science to support the new schoolwide focus. I also meet with parents monthly to collect ideas and to share upcoming academic requirements and events. Last month [October, 2018], we had our largest group of fifty-two parents; our first meeting had eight. Parents are starting to hear that their voice matters in decision making and are excited to attend parent partnerships with Principal Pinchot. (M. Pinchot, personal communication, November 12, 2018)

Productive parent partnerships are possible; we must recommit to this commonsense idea. And let's proceed with respect. According to Michelle Pinchot (personal communication, November 12, 2018):

> We can't assume that we know what parents need to be "educated" on or what they need or want for their own self-growth or for their child's. We need to ask them for their input; we need to listen. I have found that empowering parents to "early wins" encourages initial participation. Then, later, we expand involvement into other initiatives.

Michelle recognizes that involving parents as partners requires that we respect their knowledge, value and incorporate their input, and persevere with opportunities for parents to contribute, even if attendance at initial meetings is lower. These conclusions are validated in Comer's research (Comer et al., 1996).

Including Parents as Interventionists

Talman Elementary School, a K–8 school in Chicago's Pilsen neighborhood, is one of Chicago Public Schools' most creative and successful buildings. In 2014, principal Jackie Medina invited me to hear from staff about their systems of supports that have led to record-setting achievement. Early in my visit, after talking with and learning from a group of adults for twenty minutes, I discovered that the group was composed entirely of parents. Parent tutors are ever present in the school hallways and classrooms. They significantly lower adult-student ratios and provide interventions to students, serving as interventionists and providing targeted supports for students who have vulnerabilities in the areas of reading and mathematics. Additionally, this parent network is self-sustaining; after years of practice and success, parents teach and empower the next generation of parents every year.

Making Common Sense More Common

Irvine Unified School District is recommitting to common-sense ways of collaborating with families. We teachers have many strategies we can use to engage families. First, we can more proactively get to know parents and learn more about their children through *meet and greets*, in which we share how we will communicate and hear their expectations; we can then intentionally embed this information into learning environments and student goals. Drop-off and pick-up times are prime times for interacting with families; we can take advantage of these informal opportunities to exchange information and build relationships. The district's Irvine Parent Education Program provides sessions on topics of interest and importance to parents, including the district's pathways of advanced mathematics courses and health education requirements in middle and high school. Electronic gradebooks have greatly improved parents' immediate access to their children's progress; we can ensure that families know what to do with the information they access and that we are ready to respond when needs arise. We can leverage conferences more than ever to make connections with families and learn about students' strengths, interests, and identities outside school.

Like in so many school districts, well over half the families in Irvine Unified School District are non-white. We are trying to create more welcoming, open front-office spaces that present a respectful, empathetic, inclusive school culture. For example, we are including literature that reflects and includes the diverse backgrounds represented in our communities; highlighting historical contributions made by well-known and lesser-known individuals from these backgrounds; sharing the stories of role models within fields of study who reflect students' race and ethnicity; and displaying photographs of students from our schools. Last, we are continuously using school climate surveys to gather information about which aspects of school climate to prioritize.

Conclusion

Increasing parent involvement in their children's education is a goal of every school and district in which I've worked. Increasing involvement will require that we empower parents as partners in education. This chapter has described common-sense and proven approaches. We know (or could know) what to do. The question is whether we have the will to support parents so that they can even better support their children. It will take time and dedication. How do we get parents more involved in their child's education? We are the answer we've been waiting for.

Next Steps

Please complete the following next steps as you consider changes that may be appropriate for your school or district so you can help establish greater and more effective parental involvement.

1. Examine current practices by considering the following questions.
   - When asked, to what extent do parents understand how to navigate school processes and procedures?
   - When asked, to what extent do parents understand how to support their children in becoming college and career ready?
   - How impactful are your back-to-school nights, open houses, and parent information meetings? How do you know?
   - How well do parents understand schoolwide expectations of the academic and behavioral skills that all students must master?
   - To what extent do parents understand the supports that the district and school provide and how to access these supports?
   - How easily can parents access information about the needs and progress of their children?
   - How significantly involved are parents in school decision making? How do you know?

2. Discover research- and evidence-based common-sense practices by doing the following.
   - Survey parents to gather their input and opinions on key educational topics, including but not limited to their understanding of school systems and supports, their feelings about the effectiveness of district supports, and their knowledge of the key priorities to which the district and school are committed.
   - Provide meaningful opportunities for parents to be involved in their children's progress, such as student-led conferences.
   - Provide systematic and comprehensive information to all parents on the critical topics in education and with your schools (including those that parents have identified) so you build all parents' capacity to support their children to college and career readiness, with the goal that parents can ultimately facilitate these sessions.
   - Authentically involve parents in problem solving and decision making around key educational ideas, particularly areas that directly impact them, such as grades and homework.

3. Identify what you will stop doing, and develop a stop-doing plan.

4. Identify what you will start doing, and develop a start-doing plan.

Doing What Works © 2020 Solution Tree Press • SolutionTree.com
Visit **go.SolutionTree.com/leadership** to download this free reproducible.

10

Inspiring and Enabling Staff Engagement

There's no doubt that leadership is difficult, and that serving as a school principal or other school system leader can be extraordinarily challenging. The stakes are so high—human beings' futures are in development, and numerous stakeholders, understandably, demand that leaders have the answers. Despite this, trying to have all the answers may be the entirely wrong approach for leaders. They should aim for engaged and active leadership—not dictatorial and demanding behavior.

We know Newton's third law of motion: for every action, there is an equal and opposite reaction. Wise leaders will resist the temptation to push back when, inevitably, questions arise regarding continuous improvement efforts. Questioning from staff members isn't resistance; it's engagement. To illustrate the importance of this chapter's common-sense leadership practice, the following sections will detail educational practices that defy common sense, research-based best practices in education, and strategies and insights for improving student learning.

Educational Practices That Defy Common Sense

We have, I suspect, worked with and for leaders who fit into the following categories.

- **The competent manager:** The leader organizes duty schedules and back-to-school nights well. However, the leader's vision for progressive and innovative practices is not really evident.

- **The people person:** The leader is a great person with exceptional interpersonal skills. When the going gets tough or boldness is needed, however, he or she does not take decisive action.
- **The "do as I say, not as I do" boss:** The leader says impressive words, but the actions and follow-through do not match the promises.
- **The authoritarian:** The leader invokes fear as a leadership attribute.
- **The transactional leader:** The leader makes rampant changes, and things are happening. After a year, though, the staff are exhausted, and the sustainability of improvements is highly suspect.
- **The incomplete leader:** The leader has good intentions and a good energy. But shortfalls arise in vision setting, professional learning supports, resources, or incentives, or the implementation plan slowly and tragically erodes the initiative's potential benefits.
- **The door-is-closed leader:** Staff think they have a leader, but his or her door is always closed.

Having served as a site principal and district leader for well over a decade, I understand the demands of school leadership; my intent is not to pass judgment. These jobs are terrifically difficult and, frankly, I received neither adequate training nor support to be a leader. Efforts to ensure that school administrators and leaders are well versed in curriculum, instruction, budgeting, and school law are important and laudable, but how about support in the basics of leadership?

A seminal study and summary of mistakes that educational leaders make was conducted in 1998, and the lessons still apply today. Clete Bulach, Winston Pickett, and Diana Boothe (1998) identified the following fifteen categories of mistakes.

1. Poor human relations skills
2. Poor interpersonal communication skills
3. A lack of vision
4. Failure to lead
5. Avoidance of conflict
6. Lack of knowledge about instruction or curriculum
7. A control orientation
8. Lack of ethics or character
9. Lack of memory of what it is like to be a teacher
10. Inconsistency

11. Displays of favoritism
12. Failure to hold staff accountable
13. Failure to follow through
14. Snap judgments
15. Interruption of instruction with public-address-system announcements

These fifteen categories of mistakes can often be found within the types of leaders described previously. Relationally based mistakes appear most commonly.

A 2018 Gallup poll found that one of the biggest reasons that teachers leave the profession—and leave the profession early in their career—is poor site leadership and support (McFeely, 2018). Moreover, Camille Smith (2005) found that relationally astute site leadership contributed significantly to the achievement of students who, unfortunately and unnecessarily, have historically underperformed in schools.

Leadership matters. Here's what works.

Research-Based Best Practices in Education

The preponderance of research and literature on leadership portrays the ideal leader not as a dictator, but as a coach. Leaders don't order their followers to complete tasks; they collaboratively develop a vision, listen and learn with and from stakeholders, and build their teams' capacity to do the work. Leadership authors Ken Blanchard and Spencer Johnson (1982), in *The One Minute Manager*, write, "The key to successful leadership today is influence, not authority" (p. 13). Top leadership thinker John Maxwell (2007) echoes this sentiment when he says, "Leadership is influence—nothing more, nothing less" (p. 13). And business icon Jack Welch notes, "Before you are a leader, success is all about growing yourself. When you become a leader, success is all about growing others" (Welch & Welch, 2005, p. 47).

In *The Heart of Change*, John Kotter and Dan Cohen (2002) note that leaders effect positive, productive, and sustained improvements in their organizations through the people with whom they work. Leaders gather a guiding coalition, craft a clear and simple vision, empower people to overcome obstacles, and strive to maintain momentum until the change becomes the new normal. Leaders don't push the change; they guide the change.

Motivational speaker and author Simon Sinek (2009) famously encourages leaders to "start with why." What they do and how they do it will emerge from the articulation of the why of change. Starting with why requires that leaders collaboratively define the why, and then involve individuals within the organization in the change process.

In *Switch*, business and entrepreneurship specialists Chip and Dan Heath (2010) note that resistance to improvement efforts often comes from a lack of clarity. What leaders perceive as laziness often results from stress because change is moving faster than the speed of trust. Perceived problems with people are often problems with the plan. The lesson, Heath and Heath (2010) conclude, is to work with your colleagues, not against them. The vision is what's important—it defines your why. The specific actions, options, and implementation will likely emerge through the change process itself.

Of course, this thinking of the leader as a coach who empowers teams isn't new. W. Edwards Deming (2013), Peter Drucker (1990), Peter Senge (1990), and Jim Collins (2001) all reached the same conclusions. Interestingly, and not coincidentally, the principles of leader as coach merge smoothly with the principles of PLC at Work, which I explore in this book's introduction (page 1). The works of Deming (2013) and Senge (1990) are precursors to the work of DuFour and Eaker.

An exhaustive analysis of leadership in exceptional schools notes, "The most direct and impactful way principals can influence student learning is by building and maintaining a strong learning climate in their schools" (Allensworth et al., 2018, p. 26). And shaping strong learning cultures requires that principals empower others to lead. The authors of this analysis state:

> Teachers and students need support to build their leadership capacity. . . . By developing structures to build teacher leadership capacity, principals empower teachers to take ownership over moving learning goals forward. . . . This includes involving teachers in schoolwide decisions, purposefully distributing leadership responsibilities (as opposed to ad hoc task delegation) to teachers and other student support staff. (Allensworth et al., 2018, p. 26)

However, some staff members may be wary of assuming leadership responsibilities if mutual trust with their leader is missing. Indeed, trust is foundational to collaborative leadership (Bryk & Schneider, 2002).

Irvine Unified School District has taken genuine steps to put this research into action. Examples and suggestions from our experience follow.

Strategies and Insights for Improving Student Learning

Leadership is most definitely a challenge, and it represents a set of skills that people can learn and continuously improve. This profession deserves and demands that leaders possess the most refined qualities and skills. Based on the available research, I would like to propose several strategies that educator leaders at all levels should adopt to further develop their ability to influence. These leadership strategies match very well what leadership experts propose to be key to effective leadership. This section will discuss the following strategies for leaders to develop.

- Balancing instruction and empowerment
- Establishing trust
- Planning for and mitigating predictable challenges
- Leaning in
- Learning to listen, learn, influence, and persuade
- Creating a culture of growth
- Sharing and developing leadership skills

Along with examples from my own experiences at Irvine Unified School District, this section will contain words of wisdom and encouragement from experienced, influential school leaders.

Balancing Instruction and Empowerment

While someone may be the leader by position, that person will very unlikely be effective, particularly in the long term, if he or she leads by bossing people around. We, as leaders, simply don't need to have all the answers. In fact, the people with whom we work don't want us to or need us to have all the answers; they may very well have answers that are as good as our ideas. The leaders I admire display a combination of confidence, humility, and empathy, and it is this style of leadership that I try to emulate. I recommend that leaders at all levels have the confidence and humility to engage colleagues in the continuous improvement process through a partnership with colleagues and with those they supervise, in part through beginning conversations with questions. Leaders do not need to, and likely cannot, have all the answers. Through questioning, listening, pausing, and paraphrasing, leaders can coach colleagues to develop solutions. Also, leaders should recognize that all staff members are working as hard as they can, and have empathy that changes are inherently stressful.

Leaders don't need to be, and perhaps shouldn't be, bosses. Rather, leadership requires a balance between instruction and empowerment. Stan Machesky, a former teacher and principal and current executive director of elementary education in Irvine Unified School District, guides dozens of elementary schools with this balance in mind. He notes:

> Finding the sweet spot within the balance of active instructional leadership and teacher empowerment is key. Those who operate with a heavy hand in driving the actual actions taken by staff disempower staff and undervalue their input and ownership. This can be effective in the early stages and can appear successful; however, once this pattern of over-governance is established, the staff become dependent on the singular choice of their leader. On the other side, those who take their hand off the wheel of instructional leadership greatly diminish their understanding of the roads being traveled and who may be steering at any given time. Shared leadership is a fundamental belief of mine, but *shared* doesn't mean teachers and staff should have all the power. (S. Machesky, personal communication, January 26, 2019)

Establishing Trust

Relationships matter so much. In the case of relationships among educational professionals, you cannot rush continuous improvements and changes. If educator leaders at all levels do not devote time to defining the why behind the necessary shifts and to listening to concerns, questions, and suggestions from all stakeholders, then, in my experience, the changes will not succeed, and resentments may develop that dwell for years.

Irvine Unified School District recognizes that trust and transparency are inextricably linked. And the new standards and frameworks in English language arts (for example, Common Core and Texas Essential Knowledge and Skills), mathematics (for example, Common Core and Texas Essential Knowledge and Skills), science (Next Generation Science Standards), and history and social science (the College, Career, and Civic Life [C3] Framework for Social Studies State Standards) have created a need to engage school communities in continuous improvement and provided the opportunity to practice trust- and interest-based problem solving. The district leaders with whom I work have employed such practices since the 1990s.

First, they bring a group of stakeholders together from within the school district and from the surrounding community, including parents, industry professionals, and college or university experts. This stakeholder group reviews the conditions that necessitate the change; for example, in the case of new curricular frameworks, the group members define the reason for and the nature of the required change, and they share historical student data by celebrating successes and identifying opportunities for improvements.

Next, the stakeholders discuss the story of the district related to the area of change—"Where have we been, and where are we now?" Then, stakeholders identify the interests on which all agree. These are not actions or decisions on the *what* and *how*;

rather, the interests represent the ideals or *North Stars* that will guide the stakeholder committee's work and the district's decisions (the what and how) going forward. By discussing changes with the stakeholder group of teachers, administrators, parents, and community members instead of forcing change onto them, and by devoting as much time to the why as is needed, these district leaders build a firm foundation of trust with the stakeholders involved.

Planning for and Mitigating Predictable Challenges

Change is hard, whether the changes occur in our professional lives or our personal ones. In chapter 2 (page 31), I discussed the concept "If it's predictable, it's preventable," which focused on planning for student needs that we can predict. This phrase applies equally well to change. If we can predict that change will create discomfort, then let's prevent any negative outcomes we can by facilitating and leading the change in a collaborative, systematic manner.

Change can be difficult for many reasons. These include concerns with uncertainty, perceived loss of control, expected losses of one's own and the organization's efficacy, and mistrust of the change agents and the change process (Fox, Amichai-Hamburger, & Evans, 2001; Fullan, 2016). Leaders can mitigate these difficulties by successfully addressing the five elements of successful change reported by Mary Lippitt (1987).

1. **Sharing the *vision*:** When stakeholders do not clearly understand the vision and the whys of, the reasons behind, and the need for a change, confusion will occur.

2. **Ensuring that stakeholders possess the necessary *skills*:** When stakeholders do not possess the knowledge and abilities to successfully and confidently make the change, anxiety will result. Leaders must commit to initial and ongoing professional skill learning.

3. **Providing *incentives* for the change:** Leaders must highlight the ways in which students will benefit from the change and the ways that the change will enhance educators' satisfaction and effectiveness. A sometimes-forgotten incentive to change is accountability. Leaders and staff members must hold one another accountable to making changes that align to the vision. If an incentive to change does not exist, then changes and improvements will be uneven at best.

4. **Ensuring that leaders have acquired and shared the *resources* necessary to implement the change:** When resources are insufficient, then frustrations will arise.

5. **Preparing and executing an *action plan*:** A clearly communicated and well-implemented plan will help prevent false starts. The action plan should include a launch, ongoing supports, monitoring, and adjustments.

These five domains will help leaders successfully effect change. Assuming the best intentions of stakeholders, including those who ask the tough questions, is also a necessary prerequisite for ensuring authentic engagement and for mitigating predictable challenges. Irvine Unified School District has used this change paradigm to plan and manage continuous improvement efforts. Given the connections between leadership and staff and student performance, a commitment to nurturing the skills of all educator leaders in facilitating change is a very wise investment of time and resources indeed.

Leaning In

Leaders must have a willingness to walk the walk and roll up their proverbial sleeves. This essential characteristic is often accompanied by an earnest desire to discover any problems with a situation and to work with those most closely involved in order to fix things. Stan Machesky (personal communication, January 26, 2019) calls this concept *leaning in*:

> Leaders leaning into issues that present themselves and serving as active, engaged participants in what is happening in any given situation is key. As they "lean in," the acts of listening for understanding, summarizing what they are hearing, and asking deep and probing questions get to the essence of what is at hand and allow for shared outcomes and decisions to elegantly emerge. Too often we feel forced with the tyranny of the immediate or urgent, and we fall into solution thinking. This can be effective in the short term, but ultimately leads to solutions being funneled through the very few when the impact is felt on the many.

Schools deserve leaders who lean in.

Learning to Listen, Learn, Influence, and Persuade

In my experience, a leader who dictates and mandates either won't last long or will only impact short-term shifts that won't last. I believe that shortcomings in these areas often relate to incorrect, negative assumptions regarding the educators whom leaders serve. To their detriment, leaders sometimes assume that the individuals whom they lead either don't know, or worse, don't care about reflecting upon and improving practices. Leaders should assume that the individuals whom they are honored to lead possess the best intentions; this assumption or orientation will lead, quite naturally, to listening authentically to the input of others.

Keith Tuominen, Irvine Unified School District's executive director of secondary education, has observed that the interpersonal elements of leadership are vital and, at times, underdeveloped. He states:

> I think the leadership practices that are less than effective usually revolve around one of three key things: forgetting the human factor, moving too fast, or not taking the risks necessary for continuous improvement. I have seen administrators who charge forward and make decisions without realizing the impact on others. They don't take time to listen or gather input from others. Instead they make a decision and let their ego guide the way. These leaders don't practice taking on the perspective of others, and they don't build the opportunity for others to broaden their perspective. I have seen principals who present change as an obligation, meeting some requirement from the district or the state, and fail to develop ways a school team could own the change. I have seen administrators who fail to move forward with needed change because it feels too uncomfortable, requires too much work, or is too laden with risk. These principals may be managers but they are not acting as instructional leaders. They are afraid to be the courageous leader that is needed in order to support our mission to create the very best educational experience we can envision for all of our students. (K. Tuominen, personal communication, January 20, 2019)

Leaders are coaches, whether athletic coaches or cognitive coaches. As leaders, our job is to bring out the best in those we serve and those we coach. We can do this by listening to understand, by learning about all stakeholders' needs and perspectives, by summarizing and openly problem solving, and by influencing and persuading individual educators and the team to even higher performance levels. Yes, we must be patiently persistent—the stakes for students are too high for us not to be—and coaches combine patience and persistence in a blend informed by love, respect, energy, and high expectations. Listening respectfully to our colleagues and learning of their needs and ideas will enhance leaders' success in influencing and persuading.

Memorably, I forgot this lesson as a school principal in 2007 at Richard Henry Dana Elementary School. The school team had identified a goal—we needed to increase the amount of time that students spent engaged in instructional tasks—and had agreed to meet it, but my ego led me astray. I had heard of a school that had extended the school day by thirty minutes and increased potential instructional time by over two hours a week. I became myopically focused on this idea of how to meet the goal, and failed to listen and learn. I cajoled (and strong-armed) the staff and community into adopting this plan. I didn't listen, I rushed, and I definitely attempted to move faster than the speed of trust. Luckily, the amazing staff I worked with pointed out that there were concerns, even flaws, in my plan. And I finally listened. They further pointed out that other approaches would also result in us meeting our goal. Through their creativity, we did just that, and annual student achievement continued to increase significantly every year for over four years. When I shifted from dictator to coach and facilitated the change process, we effectively and happily made changes that benefited all stakeholders. Far from requiring that someone give orders to his or her subordinates, leadership is actually as collaborative as teaching.

Creating a Culture of Growth

Leaders are primary shapers of cultures. John Pehrson—a successful high school principal in Irvine Unified School District since 2005, and a high school educator for nearly three decades—notes that all leaders on a school campus have the foundational task of creating a culture in which striving for growth is the norm. He offers the following words of wisdom:

> In the absence of a vision and strong intention, culture will determine its own destiny . . . usually, the least common denominator due to human nature. People naturally gravitate to whatever requires the least amount of energy. That being said, with intention and focus on a singular vision, students receive a common message in many different ways and find it easier to go with the flow of the current than to do their own thing. A relentless pursuit toward a common goal by those in a position to lead will ultimately influence those in the organization toward that goal. A cohesive community is developed and united as it works together toward common interests and targets. (J. Pehrson, personal communication, February 5, 2019)

It's common sense: if our goal is to have engaged stakeholders, we, as leaders, must take the lead in intentionally fostering cultures of high expectations for ourselves, teachers, and students. Pehrson (personal communication, February 5, 2019) puts it this way:

> The consequence of *not* taking ownership of driving the culture or mindsets is that organizations are opened up to negative or, at best, inconsistent behaviors by the members. Different people emphasizing different things leads to confusion, isolation, and a lack of community. While individuals may thrive and rise to the top in this environment, the good of the whole group is rarely a priority.

I believe that we have as much growth to make in the art and science of leadership as we do in any other single aspect of our incredible profession. We most definitely have the capacity to make this growth. We will go a long way toward improving as leaders by increasingly viewing leadership as a collaborative endeavor.

Sharing and Developing Leadership Skills

Leadership is infinite. The job is too challenging for education to have a limited number of leaders. Administrators are leaders, teachers are leaders (of their departments, their teams, and their classrooms), and parents are leaders. (Empowering parents as partners in leadership was the focus of chapter 9, page 137.) As leaders, we must be confident and humble enough to share power; we've already got the job, so we needn't feel threatened, and the best way of keeping the job is to trust colleagues and empower the individuals with whom we work. Even if a new leader (at the district or site) could do the job alone, the more empowered an individual is, the more invested he or she should become.

Irvine Unified School District models the practice of leadership sharing in two significant ways. First, every administrator at every level receives extensive leadership professional learning opportunities at least once a month. These two- to four-hour opportunities build the capacity of the positional leaders within the district. Not surprisingly, these sessions focus on listening to, learning with, and influencing the colleagues we serve to higher levels of effectiveness. Keith Tuominen (personal communication, January 20, 2019) agrees:

> We can nurture leaders by providing opportunities to be leaders. When we put together task forces and committees that involve important and authentic objectives, we provide leadership opportunities for everyone involved. This necessitates being open to adjustments in the process and building a system that requires ownership and responsibility by everyone involved. If we invite potential leaders into the important work of our schools, we can broaden their perspectives and help build leadership skills.

Second, the district commits to shared leadership by providing monthly multihour sessions with our PLC facilitator coaches. These coaches receive release time during their days so they can lead their colleagues in the work of teaching and learning within collaborative teams. It's an example of leaders supporting leaders who support leaders—district leaders build the capacity of the PLC facilitator-coach leaders who support their teacher-leader colleagues back at their sites. Both of these district commitments to nurturing leaders invest a lot of money and time into the shared responsibility of serving our colleagues, students, and communities. According to Keith Tuominen (personal communication, January 20, 2019):

> We can also nurture leaders by providing time with mentors and by involving them in professional learning through structured programs, or through goal setting, or even through book studies done together. Within these structures, we can build the opportunities for reflection and action, giving new leaders the chance to learn how to learn with a group, and utilizing the PLC process along the way.

The legacy of PLC at Work endures in part because the concept of collaborative approaches to our work and collective responsibility for all students learning at high levels has more to it than the powerful practices that districts, schools, and teams apply. An underlying principle of PLC at Work is that team members believe in one another. Educators who fully embrace their professional responsibilities understand that leaders exist at all levels of the organization and that the educators closest to the students—teacher teams—are best positioned to make decisions—or to lead—in curriculum- and instruction-related areas. Aaron Jetzer (personal communication, February 7, 2019), one of Irvine Unified School District's outstanding elementary principals, believes that the excellence of his school rests on a "foundation of relationships and connections with students." The school builds this foundation on its emphasis on inclusive decision making for continuous improvement, as follows: "We have amazing educators—let's guide, not direct them. We first determine our North Star and then guide colleagues in their journey toward the mission" (A. Jetzer, personal communication, February 7, 2019). At Jetzer's school, personalized student learning is the North Star. He says:

> Curriculum, instruction, assessment, community partnership, the use of space and time, and personalized professional learning all serve this North Star. We have created a work environment in which we'll do whatever it takes to serve the customers, our students and families, and the status quo is not an option—there can be no excuses toward progress. (A. Jetzer, personal communication, February 7, 2019)

Conclusion

Effective leadership can and should be practiced and improved. Stan Machesky (personal communication, January 26, 2019) believes:

> Intentional, impactful, and timely reflection is essential in the maturation process of leaders. Leadership "autopsies" of the actual events occurring with our leaders provide us with true, real, emotional, and situational contexts from which to build their skills. Providing opportunities

for leaders in similar situations to share their learnings with one another can strengthen their individual maturity levels and broaden their understanding of how, what, when, and why regarding applied leadership skills and strategies.

Leading fellow educators in this most important of societal efforts—serving communities and educating students—requires a mindset that honors and encourages the contributions of all. Dictating that initiatives are implemented or requiring compliance will result in lackluster performance or defiance. When leaders facilitate change and continuous importance, and when guiding schools is truly practiced as a collaborative endeavor, staff will be authentically engaged, ownership of efforts will be elevated, implementations will be more successful, and student achievement will more likely be positively impacted. Our leadership is never more needed than when designing systems of supports that proactively prepare for all our students' anticipatable needs.

Next Steps

Please complete the following next steps as you consider changes that may be appropriate for your school or district while you attempt to lead by influencing, not dictating.

1. Examine current practices by considering the following questions.
   - Do teachers feel as if they have an authentic voice in curriculum and instruction decisions?
   - Do all staff members have a passion for which they take the lead across the school?
   - How are decisions made across the school and district?
   - In what ways has the district invested in the leadership and coaching skills of leaders across the district?
   - Has your school or district made changes about which it shared little or no information or rationale?

2. Discover research- and evidence-based common-sense practices by doing the following.
   - Make interest-based decision making the norm when exploring significant shifts and innovations.
   - Survey teachers' interests, passions, and skills, and empower staff to take a lead in serving community and student needs in an area that matches these interests.
   - Invest in the development of leaders of all kinds across the district, providing guidance and practice on coaching, active listening, and collaborative leadership.
   - Respect and prepare for the elements of change developed by Mary Lippitt and described in this chapter, have empathy toward staff's responses to change, and patiently and persistently listen, inform, and develop mutual interests.
   - Be open to the possibility that resistance and questioning are actually engagement.

3. Identify what you will stop doing, and develop a stop-doing plan.

4. Identify what you will start doing, and develop a start-doing plan.

Epilogue

Education is the most important profession in the world. Educators impact a greater percentage of people within a society than any other professionals do. The job of educating students is critically important, and literally a matter of life and death—the more educated an individual, the longer his or her life span (Olshansky et al., 2012) and the greater his or her quality of life (Ionescu, Ionescu, & Jaba, 2013).

An educational crisis does not exist; yet, educators and educator leaders can and must continuously improve our practices, approaches, and mindsets regarding who learns at all levels (all students), what is learned, and how learning best occurs. The characteristics of the students we serve have changed; the world for which we prepare students has changed as well.

This book was not intended to be either a repudiation of education and educators or a comprehensive plan for improving schools. Instead, I hope that it has been a reminder that, in many cases, we already know what to do. While new ideas and innovative practices, programs, and pedagogies are exciting, this book makes the case that the simplest practices are often the most effective—that common sense, while not as common as it ought to be, deserves our consideration. Doing more or doing new is not always necessary or the best approach.

The job of educating students with a myriad of needs is incredibly difficult; we simply cannot do it alone. PLC at Work empowers educators to learn with and from one another. According to Hattie (2009):

> Excellence in education requires that teachers work in collaborative teams to clarify the learning intentions and success criteria of their lessons, gather evidence of student learning, and discuss the effectiveness of their teaching based on that evidence. Teachers need to share evidence about their teaching with their colleagues. The key question is whether teaching can shift from an immature to mature profession, from opinions to evidence. The education profession will not mature as

a profession until professional dialogue focuses on evidence of student learning rather than opinions. (pp. 252, 259)

Professionals should authentically collaborate with one another in support of the stakeholders they serve.

I hope educators consider exploring and implementing the following practices within a foundation of a PLC at Work.

- Teaching less so students learn more, so that mastery of essential standards at the appropriate level of depth is more viable or doable

- Predicting and preventing challenges, so that the power of response to intervention and a multitiered system of supports proactively provides all students with targeted supports within an organized school plan

- Letting students do the talking and the learning, so that students are more actively engaged in their learning journey

- Keeping learning targets visible and still, so that both educators and students are crystal clear on what all students will master, and so that time and information exist to ensure that all students get to mastery

- Nurturing behavioral habits that affect motivation, so that critically important behavioral skills are prioritized alongside the academic teaching and learning that occur within schools

- Fostering two-way feedback, so that educators and students receive accurate feedback (through both formal and more informal assessments) about where students currently are, and so that educators can provide timely and specific feedback to students about how to improve

- Emphasizing skills alongside or above content, so that students can explain, interpret, and apply the important knowledge that they have acquired

- Promoting rigorous learning tasks, so that the work that educators assign students and with which they engage matches the high expectations for their performance and the realities they will face within college and skilled careers

- Empowering parents as partners in education, so that the necessary and vital links between school and home can be solidified, and so that students see their home and school families as united in their care for them and their futures

- Inspiring and enabling staff engagement, so that leadership is more distributed and the talents, skills, and experiences of more staff members impact student learning

Too many schools are suffering from initiative fatigue. This has led to our compromising the potentially positive impact of existing practices; ceasing to use effective practices that, in fact, work; and overcomplicating the already complex work of teaching and learning. We have set aside or forgotten common-sense and research-based sets of principles and practices, or we simply have not implemented them very well. The ten practices described in this book make sense and meet the predictable needs of the students we serve.

References and Resources

Ainsworth, L. (2013). *Prioritizing the Common Core: Identifying specific standards to emphasize the most*. Boston: Houghton Mifflin Harcourt.

Allensworth, E., Farrington, C. A., Gordon, M. F., Johnson, D. W., Klein, K., McDaniel, B., et al. (2018, October). *Supporting social, emotional, and academic development: Research implications for educators*. Chicago: University of Chicago Consortium on School Research.

Allington, R. L. (2011). What at-risk readers need. *Educational Leadership, 68*(6), 40–45.

Anderson, L. W., & Krathwohl, D. R. (Eds.). (2001). *A taxonomy for learning, teaching, and assessing: A revision of Bloom's taxonomy of educational objectives*. New York: Longman.

Anderson, L. W., Krathwohl, D. R., & Bloom, B. S. (2001). *A taxonomy for learning, teaching, and assessing: A revision of Bloom's taxonomy of educational objectives* (Complete ed.). New York: Longman.

Ausubel, D. P. (1968). *Educational psychology: A cognitive view*. New York: Holt, Rinehart and Winston.

Barth, R. S. (2006). Improving relationships within the schoolhouse. *Educational Leadership, 63*(6), 8–13.

Benner, G. J., Kutash, K., Nelson, J. R., & Fisher, M. B. (2013). Closing the achievement gap of youth with emotional and behavioral disorders through multi-tiered systems of support. *Education and Treatment of Children, 36*(3), 15–29.

Beyranevand, M. (2017a, November 12). *Retaking assessments: Many math teachers are late to the party!* [Blog post]. Accessed at https://medium.com/q-e-d/retaking-assessments-many-math-teachers-are-late-to-the-party-ae7a0b7e5428 on October 27, 2017.

Beyranevand, M. (2017b). *Teach math like this, not like that: Four critical areas to improve student learning*. Lanham, MD: Rowman & Littlefield.

Black, P., & Wiliam, D. (2010). Inside the black box: Raising standards through classroom assessment. *Phi Delta Kappan, 92*(1), 81–90.

Blackburn, B. R. (2014). *Rigor in your classroom: A toolkit for teachers*. New York: Routledge.

Blair, C., & Diamond, A. (2008). Biological processes in prevention and intervention: The promotion of self-regulation as a means of preventing school failure. *Development and Psychopathology, 20*(3), 899–911.

Blanchard, K., & Johnson, S. (1982). *The one minute manager.* New York: Morrow.

Bloom, B. S. (Ed.). (1956). *Taxonomy of educational objectives, handbook 1: Cognitive domain.* New York: Longman.

Bloom, B. S. (1968). Learning for mastery. Instruction and curriculum. Regional Education Laboratory for the Carolinas and Virginia, topical papers and reprints, number 1. *Evaluation Comment, 1*(2), 1–12.

Bloom, B. S. (1971). Mastery learning. In J. H. Block (Ed.), *Mastery learning: Theory and practice* (pp. 47–63). New York: Holt, Rinehart and Winston.

Bloom, B. S. (1974). Time and learning. *American Psychologist, 29*(9), 682–688.

Bloom, B. S. (1984). The search for methods of group instruction as effective as one-to-one tutoring. *Educational Leadership, 41*(8), 4–17.

Bloom, B. S., Hastings, J. T., & Madaus, G. F. (1971). *Handbook on formative and summative evaluation of student learning.* New York: McGraw-Hill.

Boaler, J. (2018, November 3). *Mindset mathematics: Teachers and students changing together.* Paper presented at the annual meeting of the California Mathematics Council–South, Palm Springs, CA.

Bordoff, J., Furman, J., & Bendor, J. (2007, February 14). *An education strategy to promote opportunity, prosperity, and growth.* Washington, DC: Brookings Institution. Accessed at www.brookings.edu/research/an-education-strategy-to-promote-opportunity-prosperity-and-growth on September 8, 2018.

Bourassa, M. (2019). *Which one doesn't belong?* Accessed at https://wodb.ca/ on January 17, 2019.

Boynton, M., & Boynton, C. (2005). *The educator's guide to preventing and solving discipline problems.* Alexandria, VA: Association for Supervision and Curriculum Development.

Bradley, R., Danielson, L., & Hallahan, D. P. (Eds.). (2002). *Identification of learning disabilities: Research to practice.* Mahwah, NJ: Lawrence Erlbaum.

Brown, P. C., Roediger, H. L., & McDaniel, M. A (2014). *Make it stick: The science of successful learning.* Cambridge, MA: Belknap Press.

Bryk, A. S., & Schneider, B. (2002). *Trust in schools: A core resource for improvement.* New York: Russell Sage Foundation.

Bryk, A. S., Sebring, P. B., Allensworth, E., Luppescu, S., & Easton, J. Q. (2010). *Organizing schools for improvement: Lessons from Chicago.* Chicago: University of Chicago Press.

Buffum, A., Hierck, T., Mattos, M., & Weber, C. (2015). *Uniting academic and behavior interventions: Solving the skill or will dilemma.* Bloomington, IN: Solution Tree Press.

Buffum, A., Mattos, M., & Weber, C. (2009). *Pyramid response to intervention: RTI, professional learning communities, and how to respond when kids don't learn*. Bloomington, IN: Solution Tree Press.

Buffum, A., Mattos, M., & Weber, C. (2010). The why behind RTI. *Educational Leadership*, *68*(2), 10–16.

Buffum, A., Mattos, M., & Weber, C. (2011). *Simplifying response to intervention: Four essential guiding principles*. Bloomington, IN: Solution Tree Press.

Buffum, A., Mattos, M., Weber, C., & Hierck, T. (2015). *Uniting academic and behavior interventions: Solving the skill or will dilemma*. Bloomington, IN: Solution Tree Press.

Bulach, C., Pickett, W., & Boothe, D. (1998). *Mistakes educational leaders make*. Accessed at Eric.ed.gov on September 16, 2019.

Burns, M. K., Appleton, J. J., & Stehouwer, J. D. (2005). Meta-analytic review of responsiveness-to-intervention research: Examining field-based and research-implemented models. *Journal of Psychoeducational Assessment*, *23*(4), 381–394.

Burns, M. K., & Symington, T. (2002). A meta-analysis of prereferral intervention teams: Student and systemic outcomes. *Journal of School Psychology*, *40*(5), 437–447.

California Department of Education. (1998). *History–social science content standards for California public schools: Kindergarten through grade twelve*. Sacramento, CA: Author.

Carnevale, A. P., Smith, N., & Strohl, J. (2010). *Help wanted: Projections of jobs and education requirements through 2018*. Washington, DC: Georgetown University Center on Education and the Workforce. Accessed at https://cew.georgetown.edu/cew-reports/help-wanted on September 8, 2018.

Carnevale, A. P., Smith, N., & Strohl, J. (2012). *Recovery: Job growth and education requirements through 2020*. Washington, DC: Georgetown University Center on Education and the Workforce. Accessed at https://cew.georgetown.edu/cew-reports/recovery-job-growth-and-education-requirements-through-2020 on September 8, 2018.

Chappuis, J. (2005). Helping students understand assessment. *Educational Leadership*, *63*(3), 39–43.

Chappuis, J., & Stiggins, R. (2017). *An introduction to student-involved assessment* for *learning* (7th ed.). Columbus, OH: Pearson.

Chappuis, J., Stiggins, R., Chappuis, S., & Arter, J. (2012). *Classroom assessment* for *student learning: Doing it right—using it well* (2nd ed.). Boston, MA: Pearson.

City, E. A., Elmore, R. F., Fiarman, S. E., & Teitel, L. (2009). *Instructional rounds in education: A network approach to improving teaching and learning*. Cambridge, MA: Harvard Education Press.

Clark, R. C., &. Mayer, R. E. (2008). Learning by viewing versus learning by doing: Evidence-based guidelines for principled learning environments. *Performance Improvement, 47*(9), 5–13.

Colby, R. L. (2017). *Competency-based education: A new architecture for K–12 schooling.* Cambridge, MA: Harvard Education Press.

College Board. (2014, February). *The 10th annual AP report to the nation.* New York: Author. Accessed at http://media.collegeboard.com/digitalServices/pdf/ap/rtn/10th-annual/10th-annual-ap-report-to-the-nation-single-page.pdf on March 20, 2015.

College Board. (2018). *AP course and exam redesign.* Accessed at https://aphighered.collegeboard.org/courses-exams/course-exam-redesign on November 12, 2018.

Collins, J. (2001). *Good to great: Why some companies make the leap . . . and others don't.* New York: HarperBusiness.

Collins, J., & Porras, J. I. (2004). *Built to last: Successful habits of visionary companies.* New York: HarperBusiness.

Comer, J. P., Haynes, N. M., Joyner, E. T., & Ben-Avie, M. (Eds.). (1996). *Rallying the whole village: The Comer process for reforming education.* New York: Teachers College Press.

Conley, D. T. (2014). *Getting ready for college, careers, and the Common Core: What every educator needs to know.* San Francisco: Jossey-Bass.

Costa, A. L., & Kallick, B. (2000). *Habits of mind: A developmental series.* Alexandria, VA: Association for Supervision and Curriculum Development.

Daggett, W. R. (2016). *Rigor, relevance, and relationships in action: Innovative leadership and best practices for rapid school improvement.* Rexford, NY: International Center for Leadership in Education.

Danielson, C. (2008). *The handbook for enhancing professional practice: Using the framework for teaching in your school.* Alexandria, VA: Association for Supervision and Curriculum Development.

DeAngelis, K. J., & Presley, J. B. (2011). Toward a more nuanced understanding of new teacher attrition. *Education and Urban Society, 43*(5), 598–626.

Deci, E. L. (1992). The relation of interest to the motivation of behavior: A self-determination theory perspective. In K. A. Renninger, S. Hidi, & A. Krapp (Eds.), *The role of interest in learning and development* (pp. 43–71). Hillsdale, NJ: Erlbaum.

Deming, D. J. (2015). *The growing importance of social skills in the labor market* (NBER Working Paper No. 21473). Cambridge, MA: National Bureau of Economic Research.

Deming, W. E. (2013). *The essential Deming: Leadership principles from the father of quality* (J. N. Orsini, Ed.). New York: McGraw-Hill.

Dougherty, D., & Conrad, A. (2016). *Free to make: How the maker movement is changing our schools, our jobs, and our minds.* Berkeley, CA: North Atlantic Books.

Drucker, P. F. (1990). Lesson for successful nonprofit governance. *Nonprofit Management and Leadership, 1*(1), 7–14.

Duckworth, A. L. (2016). *Grit: The power of passion and perseverance.* New York: Scribner.

Duckworth, A. L., & Carlson, S. M. (2013). Self-regulation and school success. In B. W. Sokol, F. M. E. Grouzet, & U. Müller (Eds.), *Self-regulation and autonomy: Social and developmental dimensions of human conduct* (pp. 208–230). New York: Cambridge University Press.

Duckworth, A. L., Quinn, P. D., & Tsukayama, E. (2012). What No Child Left Behind leaves behind: The roles of IQ and self-control in predicting standardized achievement test scores and report card grades. *Journal of Educational Psychology, 104*(2), 439–451.

Duckworth, A. L., & Seligman, M. E. P. (2005). Self-discipline outdoes IQ in predicting academic performance of adolescents. *Psychological Science, 16*(12), 939–944.

DuFour, R. (2004). What is a professional learning community? *Educational Leadership, 61*(8), 6–11.

DuFour, R. (2015). *In praise of American educators: And how they can become even better.* Bloomington, IN: Solution Tree Press.

DuFour, R., DuFour, R., Eaker, R., & Karhanek, G. (2004). *Whatever it takes: How professional learning communities respond when kids don't learn.* Bloomington, IN: Solution Tree Press.

DuFour, R., DuFour, R., Eaker, R., & Many, T. (2010). *Learning by doing: A handbook for Professional Learning Communities at Work* (2nd ed.). Bloomington, IN: Solution Tree Press.

DuFour, R., DuFour, R., Eaker, R., Many, T., & Mattos, M. (2016). *Learning by doing: A handbook for Professional Learning Communities at Work* (3rd ed.). Bloomington, IN: Solution Tree Press.

DuFour, R., Eaker, R., & DuFour, R. (2005). Closing the knowing-doing gap. In R. DuFour, R. Eaker, & R. DuFour (Eds.), *On common ground: The power of professional learning communities* (pp. 225–254). Bloomington, IN: Solution Tree Press.

Dunlosky, J., Rawson, K. A., Marsh, E. J., Nathan, M. J., & Willingham, D. T. (2013). Improving students' learning with effective learning techniques promising directions from cognitive and educational psychology. *Psychological Science in the Public Interest, 14*(1), 4–58.

Dweck, C. S. (2006). *Mindset: The new psychology of success.* New York: Random House.

Dweck, C. S., Walton, G. M., & Cohen, G. L. (2014). *Academic tenacity: Mindsets and skills that promote long-term learning.* Seattle, WA: Bill & Melinda Gates Foundation.

Edmonds, R. (1979). Effective schools for the urban poor. *Educational Leadership, 37*(1), 15–18, 20–24.

Edsall, T. B. (2012, March 12). *The reproduction of privilege* [Blog post]. Accessed at https://campaignstops.blogs.nytimes.com/2012/03/12/the-reproduction-of-privilege on September 8, 2018.

Education Week. (2014, June 5). Diplomas count 2014: Motivation matters—Engaging students, creating learners. Accessed at www.edweek.org/ew/toc/2014/06/05/index.html on January 19, 2015.

Elbaum, B., Vaughn, S., Hughes, M. T., & Moody, S. W. (2000). How effective are one-to-one tutoring programs in reading for elementary students at risk for reading failure? A meta-analysis of the intervention research. *Journal of Educational Psychology, 92*(4), 605–619.

Farrington, C. A., Roderick, M., Allensworth, E., Nagaoka, J., Keyes, T. S., Johnson, D. W., et al. (2012, June). *Teaching adolescents to become learners: The role of noncognitive factors in shaping school performance—A critical literature review.* Chicago: University of Chicago Consortium on School Research.

Fisher, D., & Frey, N. (2008). *Better learning through structured teaching: A framework for the gradual release of responsibility.* Alexandria, VA: Association for Supervision and Curriculum Development.

Fox, S., Amichai-Hamburger, Y., & Evans, E. A. (2001). The power of emotional appeals in promoting organizational change programs. *Academy of Management Executive, 15*(4), 84–95.

Freeman, S., Eddy, S. L., McDonough, M., Smith, M. K., Okoroafor, N., Jordt, H., & Wenderoth, M. P. (2014). Active learning increases student performance in science, engineering, and mathematics. *Proceedings of the National Academy of Sciences of the United States of America, 11*(23), 8410–8415.

Fullan, M. (2000). The three stories of education reform. *Phi Delta Kappan, 81*(8), 581–584.

Fullan, M. (2005). *Leadership and sustainability: System thinkers in action.* Thousand Oaks, CA: Corwin Press.

Fullan, M. (2010). *Motion leadership: The skinny on becoming change savvy.* Thousand Oaks, CA: Corwin Press.

Fullan, M. (2016). *The new meaning of educational change* (5th ed.). New York: Teachers College Press.

Fullan, M., & Pinchot, M. (2018). The fast track to sustainable turnaround. *Educational Leadership, 75*(6), 48–54.

Gersten, R., Beckmann, S., Clarke, B., Foegen, A., Marsh, L., Star, J. R., et al. (2009a). *Assisting students struggling with mathematics: Response to intervention (RTI) for elementary and middle schools* (NCEE 2009–4060). Washington, DC: National Center for Education Evaluation and Regional Assistance.

Gersten, R., Compton, D., Connor, C. M., Dimino, J., Santoro, L., Linan-Thompson, S., et al. (2009b). *Assisting students struggling with reading: Response to intervention (RTI) and multi-tier intervention in the primary grades* (NCEE 2009–4045). Washington, DC: National Center for Education Evaluation and Regional Assistance, Institute of Education Sciences, U.S. Department of Education.

Greenstone, M., Looney, A., Patashnik, J., & Yu, M. (2013, June 26). *Thirteen economic facts about social mobility and the role of education.* Washington, DC: Brookings Institution. Accessed at www.brookings.edu/research/thirteen-economic-facts-about-social-mobility-and-the-role-of-education on September 8, 2018.

Guskey, T. R. (2005). *Formative classroom assessment and Benjamin S. Bloom: Theory, research, and implications.* Paper presented at the annual meeting of the American Educational Research Association, Montréal, Québec, Canada.

Guskey, T. R. (2010). Lessons of mastery learning. *Educational Leadership, 68*(2), 52–57.

Hattie, J. (2009). *Visible learning: A synthesis of over 800 meta-analyses relating to achievement.* New York: Routledge.

Hattie, J. (2012). *Visible learning for teachers: Maximizing impact on learning.* New York: Routledge.

Hattie, J. (2019). *Collective teacher efficacy (CTE) according to John Hattie.* Accessed at https://visible-learning.org/2018/03/collective-teacher-efficacy-hattie/ on January 24, 2019.

Hattie, J., Biggs, J., & Purdie, N. (1996). Effects of learning skills interventions on student learning: A meta-analysis. *Review of Educational Research, 66*(2), 99–136.

Hattie, J., & Timperley, H. (2007). The power of feedback. *Review of Educational Research, 77*(1), 81–112.

Hattie, J., & Yates, G. C. R. (2014). *Visible learning and the science of how we learn.* New York: Routledge.

Heath, C., & Heath, D. (2010). *Switch: How to change things when change is hard.* New York: Broadway Books.

Heckman, J. J., & Kautz, T. (2012). Hard evidence on soft skills. *Labour Economics, 19*(4), 451–464.

Hierck, T., Coleman, C., & Weber, C. (2011). *Pyramid of behavior interventions: Seven keys to a positive learning environment.* Bloomington, IN: Solution Tree Press.

Hollister, R., & Watkins, M. D. (2018). Too many projects. *Harvard Business Review, 96*(5), 64–71.

Huffman, J. B., & Jacobson, A. L. (2003). Perceptions of professional learning communities. *International Journal of Leadership in Education, 6*(3), 239–250.

Ionescu, D. D., Ionescu, A. M., & Jaba, E. (2013). The investments in education and quality of life. *Journal of Knowledge Management, Economics and Information Technology, 3*(6), 141–158. Accessed at www.scientificpapers.org/wp-content/files/12_Ionescu_Jaba-THE_INVESTMENTS_IN_EDUCATION_AND_QUALITY_OF_LIFE.pdf on October 27, 2018.

Jacobs, G. M., Power, M. A., & Inn, L. W. (2002). *The teacher's sourcebook for cooperative learning: Practical techniques, basic principles, and frequently asked questions.* Thousand Oaks, CA: Corwin Press.

Jensen, E. (2009). *Teaching with poverty in mind: What being poor does to kids' brains and what schools can do about it.* Alexandria, VA: Association for Supervision and Curriculum Development.

Jensen, E. (2013). *Engaging students with poverty in mind: Practical strategies for raising achievement.* Alexandria, VA: Association for Supervision and Curriculum Development.

Jimerson, J. R., Burns, M. K., & VanDerHeyden, A. M. (2016). *Handbook of response to intervention: The science and practice of multi-tiered systems of support.* New York: Springer.

Kagan, S., & Kagan, M. (2009). *Kagan cooperative learning.* San Clemente, CA: Kagan.

Kaplan, S. N., Gould, B., & Siegel, V. (1995). *The flip book: A quick and easy method for developing differentiated learning experiences.* Calabasas, CA: Educator to Educator.

Klem, A. M., & Connell, J. P. (2004). Relationships matter: Linking teacher support to student engagement and achievement. *Journal of School Health, 74*(7), 262–273.

Kotter, J. P., & Cohen, D. S. (2002). *The heart of change: Real-life stories of how people change their organizations.* Boston: Harvard Business School Press.

Langer, J. A. (2000). Excellence in English in middle and high school: How teachers' professional lives support student achievement. *American Educational Research Journal, 37*(2), 397–439.

Larmer, J., Mergendoller, J., & Boss, S. (2015). *Setting the standard for project-based learning: A proven approach to rigorous classroom instruction.* Alexandria, VA: Association for Supervision and Curriculum Development.

Leahy, S., Lyon, C., Thompson, M., & Wiliam, D. (2005). Classroom assessment: Minute by minute, day by day. *Educational Leadership, 63*(3), 18–24.

Lee, J. S. (2014). The relationship between student engagement and academic performance: Is it a myth or reality? *Journal of Educational Research, 107*(3), 177–185.

Lezotte, L. W., & Snyder, K. M. (2010). *What effective schools do: Re-envisioning the correlates.* Bloomington, IN: Solution Tree Press.

Lippitt, M. (1987). *The managing complex change model.* Palm Harbor, FL: Enterprise Management.

MacKenzie, T. (2016). *Dive into inquiry: Amplify learning and empower student voice.* Irvine, CA: EdTechTeam Press.

Martens, B. K., & Meller, P. J. (1990). The application of behavioral principles to educational settings. In T. B. Gutkin & C. R. Reynolds (Eds.), *The handbook of school psychology* (2nd ed., pp. 612–634). New York: Wiley & Sons.

Marzano, R. J. (2003). *What works in schools: Translating research into action.* Alexandria, VA: Association for Supervision and Curriculum Development.

Marzano, R. J. (2007). *The art and science of teaching: A comprehensive framework for effective instruction.* Alexandria, VA: Association for Supervision and Curriculum Development.

Marzano, R. J. (2009). *Designing and teaching learning goals and objectives.* Bloomington, IN: Marzano Resources.

Marzano, R. J. (2017). *The new art and science of teaching.* Bloomington, IN: Solution Tree Press.

Marzano, R. J., Pickering, D. J., & Pollock, J. E. (2001). *Classroom instruction that works: Research-based strategies for increasing student achievement.* Alexandria, VA: Association for Supervision and Curriculum Development.

Maslow, A. H. (1943). A theory of human motivation. *Psychological Review, 50*(4), 370–396.

Maslow, A. H. (1954). *Motivation and personality.* New York: Harper & Row.

Mathes, P. G., Denton, C. A., Fletcher, J. M., Anthony, J. L., Francis, D. J., & Schatschneider, C. (2005). The effects of theoretically different instruction and student characteristics on the skills of struggling readers. *Reading Research Quarterly, 40*(2), 148–182.

Maxwell, J. C. (2007). *The 21 irrefutable laws of leadership: Follow them and people will follow you* (10th anniversary ed.). Nashville, TN: Thomas Nelson.

McFeely, S. (2018). *Why your best teachers are leaving and 4 ways to keep them.* Washington, DC: Gallup.

Meyer, A., Rose, D. H., & Gordon, D. (2014). *Universal design for learning: Theory and practice.* Wakefield, MA: CAST Professional.

Mischel, W. (2014). *The marshmallow test: Mastering self-control.* New York: Little, Brown.

Morris, A. K., Hiebert, J., & Spitzer, S. M. (2009). Mathematical knowledge for teaching in planning and evaluating instruction: What can preservice teachers learn? *Journal for Research in Mathematics Education, 40*(5), 491–529.

Moss, C. M., & Brookhart, S. M. (2009). *Advancing formative assessment in every classroom: A guide for instructional leaders*. Alexandria, VA: Association for Supervision and Curriculum Development.

Muhammad, A. (2018). *Transforming school culture: How to overcome staff division* (2nd ed.). Bloomington, IN: Solution Tree Press.

Mullet, J. H. (2014). Restorative discipline: From getting even to getting well. *Children and Schools, 36*(3), 157–162.

Mullis, I. V. S., Martin, M. O., Foy, P., & Arora, A. (2012). *TIMSS 2011 international results in mathematics*. Chestnut Hill, MA: Trends in International Mathematics and Science Study and Progress in International Reading Literacy Study International Study Center. Accessed at http://timssandpirls.bc.edu/timss2011/downloads/T11_IR_Mathematics_FullBook.pdf on March 20, 2015.

National Center for Education Statistics. (2019). *English language learners in public schools*. Accessed at https://nces.ed.gov/programs/coe/indicator_cgf.asp on June 24, 2019.

National Commission on Excellence in Education. (1983). *A nation at risk: The imperative for educational reform—An open letter to the American people, a report to the nation and the Secretary of Education*. Washington, DC: Author.

National Council for the Social Studies. (2013). *College, Career, and Civic Life (C3) Framework for Social Studies State Standards: Guidance for enhancing the rigor of K–12 civics, economics, geography, and history*. Silver Spring, MD: Author.

National Governors Association Center for Best Practices & Council of Chief State School Officers. (2010a). *Common Core State Standards for English language arts and literacy in history/social studies, science, and technical subjects*. Washington, DC: Authors. Accessed at www.corestandards.org/assets/CCSSI_ELA%20Standards.pdf on January 26, 2018.

National Governors Association Center for Best Practices & Council of Chief State School Officers. (2010b). *Common Core State Standards for mathematics*. Washington, DC: Authors. Accessed at www.corestandards.org/assets/CCSSI_Math%20Standards.pdf on January 26, 2018.

National Mathematics Advisory Panel. (2008). *Foundations for success: The final report of the National Mathematics Advisory Panel*. Washington, DC: U.S. Department of Education.

National Reading Panel. (2000, April). *Teaching children to read: An evidence-based assessment of the scientific research literature on reading and its implications for reading instruction*. Bethesda, MD: Author.

National Research Council. (2000). *How people learn: Brain, mind, experience, and school* (Expanded ed.). Washington, DC: National Academies Press.

New American High Schools. (2000, February). *Promising initiatives to improve education in your community*. Accessed at www.ed.gov/pubs/promisinginitiatives/nahs.html on April 23, 2006.

NGSS Lead States. (2013). *Next Generation Science Standards: For states, by states*. Washington, DC: National Academies Press.

O'Connor, E., & McCartney, K. (2007). Examining teacher–child relationships and achievement as part of an ecological model of development. *American Educational Research Journal, 44*(2), 340–369.

Olshansky, S. J., Antonucci, T., Berkman, L., Binstock, R. H., Boersch-Supan, A., Cacioppo, J. T., et al. (2012). Differences in life expectancy due to race and educational differences are widening, and many may not catch up. *Health Affairs, 31*(8), 1803–1813. Accessed at www.healthaffairs.org/doi/abs/10.1377/hlthaff.2011.0746 on October 27, 2018.

Orange County Business Council. (2019). *10 educational commandments*. Accessed at www.ocbc.org/ocbc-initiatives/lea/ on February 12, 2019.

Organisation for Economic Co-operation and Development. (2013). How the quality of the learning environment is shaped. In *What makes schools successful? Resources, policies and practices* (Vol. 4, pp. 165–188). Paris: Author. Accessed at www.oecd.org/pisa/keyfindings/Vol4Ch5.pdf on November 6, 2014.

Organisation for Economic Co-operation and Development. (2014). *CO2.2: Child poverty*. Accessed at www.oecd.org/els/CO_2_2_Child_Poverty.pdf on June 24, 2019.

Partnership for 21st Century Learning. (2019). *Framework for 21st century learning*. Accessed at www.battelleforkids.org/networks/p21/frameworks-resources on April 29, 2019.

Pfaff, M. E. (2000, April). *The effects on teacher efficacy of school-based collaborative activities structured as professional study groups*. Paper presented at the annual meeting of the American Educational Research Association, New Orleans, LA.

Phi Delta Kappa. (2014). *PDK polls of the public's attitudes toward the public schools*. Accessed at www.pdkmembers.org/members_online/publications/GallupPoll/k_q_quality_1.htm#506 on March 20, 2015.

Phillips, G., & Smith, P. (2010). Closing the gaps: Literacy for the hardest-to-teach. In P. H. Johnston (Ed.), *RTI in literacy: Responsive and comprehensive* (pp. 219–246). Newark, DE: International Reading Association.

Pinchot, M., & Weber, C. (2016). We're all in this together: Teacher empowerment and leadership transform an elementary school community. *Journal of Staff Development, 37*(5), 42–45.

Pintrich, P. R., & Schunk, D. H. (2002). *Motivation in education: Theory, research, and applications* (2nd ed.). Upper Saddle River, NJ: Prentice Hall.

Popham, W. J. (2008). *Transformative assessment*. Alexandria, VA: Association for Supervision and Curriculum Development.

Popham, W. J. (2013). *Classroom assessment: What teachers need to know* (7th ed.). Columbus, OH: Pearson.

Popham, W. J. (2018, July 19). *Our no. 1 assessment option: Prioritize or pretend?* Accessed at http://inservice.ascd.org/our-no-1-assessment-option-prioritize-or-pretend on October 14, 2018.

Poropat, A. E. (2009). A meta-analysis of the five-factor model of personality and academic performance. *Psychological Bulletin, 135*(2), 322–338.

Rampey, B. D., Dion, G. S., & Donahue, P. L. (2009, April). *National Assessment of Educational Progress 2008 trends in academic progress* (NCES 2009–479). Washington, DC: National Center for Education Statistics.

Ravitch, D. (2014). *Reign of error: The hoax of the privatization movement and the danger to America's public schools.* New York: Vintage Books.

Reddy, R., Rhodes, J. E., & Mulhall, P. (2003). The influence of teacher support on student adjustment in the middle school years: A latent growth curve study. *Development and Psychopathology, 15*(1), 119–138.

Reeves, D. (1996). *Making standards work: How to implement standards-based assessments in the classroom, school, and district.* Denver, CO: Center for Performance Assessment.

Reeves, D. (2000). *Accountability in action: A blueprint for learning organizations.* Denver, CO: Center for Performance Assessment.

Reeves, D. (2006). *The learning leader: How to focus school improvement for better results.* Alexandria, VA: Association for Supervision and Curriculum Development.

Reeves, D. (2011). *Finding your leadership focus: What matters most for student results.* New York: Teachers College Press.

Reeves, D. (2014, October 1). *Power standards* [Blog post]. Accessed at www.creativeleadership.net/blog/2014/10/1/next-generation-accountability on October 14, 2018.

Rosenholtz, S. J. (1991). *Teachers' workplace: The social organization of schools.* New York: Teachers College Press.

Rothstein, D., & Santana, L. (2011). *Make just one change: Teach students to ask their own questions.* Cambridge, MA: Harvard Education Press.

Ryan, R. M., & Deci, E. L. (2000). Intrinsic and extrinsic motivations: Classic definitions and new directions. *Contemporary Educational Psychology, 25*(1), 54–67.

Sampson, V., Enderle, P., Gleim, L., Grooms, J., Hester, M., Southerland, S., & Wilson, K. (2014). *Argument-driven inquiry in biology.* Arlington, VA: National Science Teachers Association.

Scanlon, D. M., Gelzheiser, L. M., Vellutino, F. R., Schatschneider, C., & Sweeney, J. M. (2010). Reducing the incidence of early reading difficulties: Professional development for classroom teachers versus direct interventions for children. In P. H. Johnston (Ed.), *RTI in literacy: Responsive and comprehensive* (pp. 257–291). Newark, DE: International Reading Association.

Scanlon, D. M., & Vellutino, F. R. (1997). A comparison of the instructional backgrounds and cognitive profiles of poor, average, and good readers who were initially identified as at risk for reading failure. *Scientific Studies of Reading, 1*(3), 191–215.

Schanzenbach, D. W., Nunn, R., Bauer, L., Mumford, M., & Breitwieser, A. (2016). *Seven facts on noncognitive skills from education to the labor market*. Washington, DC: Brookings Institution.

Scherer, M. (2001). How and why standards can improve student achievement: A conversation with Robert J. Marzano. *Educational Leadership, 59*(1), 14–18.

Schimmer, T. (2016). *Grading from the inside out: Bringing accuracy to student assessment through a standards-based mindset*. Bloomington, IN: Solution Tree Press.

Schmoker, M. (1999). *Results: The key to continuous school improvement* (2nd ed.). Alexandria, VA: Association for Supervision and Curriculum Development.

Schmoker, M. (2004). At odds: Strategic planning—learning communities at the crossroads—toward the best schools we've ever had. *Phi Delta Kappan, 86*(1), 84–89.

Schmoker, M. (2014). Why make reform so complicated? *Education Week, 33*(17), 22–28. Accessed at https://www.edweek.org/ew/articles/2014/01/15/17schmoker_ep.h33.html on October 14, 2018.

Schmoker, M. (2018). *Focus: Elevating the essentials to radically improve student learning* (2nd ed.). Alexandria, VA: Association for Supervision and Curriculum Development.

Seidel, T., Rimmele, R., & Prenzel, M. (2005). Clarity and coherence of lesson goals as a scaffold for student learning. *Learning and Instruction, 15*(6), 539–556.

Senge, P. M. (1990). *The fifth discipline: The art and practice of the learning organization*. New York: Doubleday/Currency.

Senge, P. M. (2000). Give me a lever long enough . . . and single-handed I can move the world. In *The Jossey-Bass reader on educational leadership* (pp. 13–25). San Francisco: Jossey-Bass.

Senge, P. M., Ross, R. B., Smith, B. J., Roberts, C., & Kleiner, A. (1994). *The fifth discipline fieldbook: Strategies and tools for building a learning organization*. New York: Doubleday.

Shaywitz, S. E. (2003). *Overcoming dyslexia: A new and complete science-based program for reading problems at any level*. New York: Random House.

Sinek, S. (2009). *Start with why: How great leaders inspire everyone to take action*. New York: Penguin.

Slavin, R. (2018, April 5). *New findings on tutoring: Four shockers* [Blog post]. Accessed at https://robertslavinsblog.wordpress.com/2018/04/05/new-findings-on-tutoring-four-shockers on September 9, 2018.

Smith, C. A. (2005). School factors that contribute to the underachievement of students of color and what culturally competent school leaders can do. *Educational Leadership and Administration, 17*, 21–32.

Sousa, D. A., & Tomlinson, C. A. (2011). *Differentiation and the brain: How neuroscience supports the learner-friendly classroom.* Bloomington, IN: Solution Tree Press.

Sousa, D. A., & Tomlinson, C. A. (2018). *Differentiation and the brain: How neuroscience supports the learner-friendly classroom* (2nd ed.). Bloomington, IN: Solution Tree Press.

Spencer, J., & Juliani, A. J. (2017). *Empower: What happens when students own their learning.* San Diego, CA: IMpress.

Sprick, R. S., Borgmeier, C., & Nolet, V. (2002). Prevention and management of behavior problems in secondary schools. In M. A. Shinn, H. M. Walker, & G. Stoner (Eds.), *Interventions for academic and behavior problems II: Preventive and remedial approaches* (pp. 373–401). Bethesda, MD: National Association of School Psychologists.

Stiggins, R. (2006). Assessment *for* learning: A key to motivation and achievement. *Edge, 2*(2), 3–19.

Stiggins, R., & DuFour, R. (2009). Maximizing the power of formative assessments. *Phi Delta Kappan, 90*(9), 640–644.

Stipek, D. J. (1988). *Motivation to learn: From theory to practice.* Englewood Cliffs, NJ: Prentice Hall.

Strahan, D. (2003). Promoting a collaborative professional culture in three elementary schools that have beaten the odds. *Elementary School Journal, 104*(2), 127–146.

Sugai, G. (2001, June 23). *School climate and discipline: Schoolwide positive behavior support.* Keynote presentation to and paper for the National Summit on the Shared Implementation of IDEA, Washington, DC.

Sugai, G., & Horner, R. (2002). The evolution of discipline practices: School-wide positive behavior supports. *Child and Family Behavior Therapy, 24*(1–2), 23–50.

Suitts, S. (2015). *A new majority research bulletin: Low income students now a majority in the nation's public schools.* Atlanta, GA: Southern Education Foundation.

Swanson, H. L., & Sachse-Lee, C. (2000). A meta-analysis of single-subject-design intervention research for students with LD. *Journal of Learning Disabilities, 33*(2), 114–136.

Tabary, Z. (2015, April 20). *The skills agenda: Preparing students for the future* [Blog post]. Accessed at www.eiuperspectives.economist.com/talent-education/driving-skills-agenda/blog/skills-agenda-preparing-students-future on November 27, 2017.

Tan, K. H. K., Tan, C., & Chua, J. S. M. (2008). The 'Teach Less, Learn More' initiative in Singapore schools. In J. E. Larkley & V. B. Maynhard (Eds.), *Innovation in education* (pp. 153–171). New York: Nova Science.

Tate, M. (2016). *Worksheets don't grow dendrites*. Thousand Oaks, CA: Corwin Press.

Thompson, S. C., Gregg, L., & Niska, J. M. (2004). Professional learning communities, leadership, and student learning. *Research in Middle Level Education, 28*(1), 1–15.

Tomlinson, C. A. (2001). *How to differentiate instruction in mixed-ability classrooms* (2nd ed.). Alexandria, VA: Association for Supervision and Curriculum Development.

Tough, P. (2012). *How children succeed: Grit, curiosity, and the hidden power of character*. Boston: Houghton Mifflin Harcourt.

Tough, P. (2016). *Helping children succeed: What works and why*. Boston: Houghton Mifflin Harcourt.

VanDerHeyden, A. M., Witt, J. C., & Gilbertson, D. A. (2007). A multiyear evaluation of the effects of a response to intervention (RTI) model on identification of children for special education. *Journal of School Psychology, 45*(2), 225–256.

Vellutino, F. R., Scanlon, D. M., Zhang, H., & Schatschneider, C. (2008). Using response to kindergarten and first grade intervention to identify children at-risk for long-term reading difficulties. *Reading and Writing, 21*(4), 437–480.

Vygotsky, L. S. (1978). *Mind in society: The development of higher psychological processes*. Cambridge, MA: Harvard University Press.

Walton, G. M., & Cohen, G. L. (2007). A question of belonging: Race, social fit, and achievement. *Journal of Personality and Social Psychology, 92*(1), 82–96.

Walton, G. M., & Cohen, G. L. (2011). A brief social-belonging intervention improves academic and health outcomes of minority students. *Science, 331*(6023), 1447–1451.

Webb, N. L. (1997, April). *Criteria for alignment of expectations and assessments on mathematics and science education* (Research Monograph No. 8). Washington, DC: Council of Chief State School Officers.

Weber, C. (2013, October 30). *Assessment (test) is not a four-letter word* [Blog post]. Accessed at www.chriswebereducation.com/easyblog/entry/assessment-test-is-a-not-a-four-letter-word on May 13, 2019.

Weber, C. (2014). *Effective, scaffolded instruction to support RTI*. Boston, MA: Houghton Mifflin Harcourt.

Weber, C. (2015). Creating consistency and collective responsibility. In A. Buffum & M. Mattos (Eds.), *It's about time: Planning interventions and extensions in elementary school* (pp. 225–253). Bloomington, IN: Solution Tree Press.

Weber, C. (2016, November). *Learning for all: Leadership is courage in action* [Blog post]. Accessed at http://blog.leadered.com/2016/11/learning-for-all-leadership-is-courage.html on May 7, 2019.

Weber, C. (2018). *Behavior: The forgotten curriculum—An RTI approach for nurturing essential life skills*. Bloomington, IN: Solution Tree Press.

Welch, J., & Welch, S. (2005). *Winning.* New York: HarperBusiness.

Wiggins, G., & McTighe, J. (1998). *Understanding by design.* Alexandria, VA: Association for Supervision and Curriculum Development.

Wiliam, D. (2018). *Embedded formative assessment* (2nd ed.). Bloomington, IN: Solution Tree Press.

Yeager, D. S., & Walton, G. (2011). Social-psychological interventions in education: They're not magic. *Review of Educational Research, 81*(2), 267–301.

Zimmerman, B. J. (2001). Theories of self-regulated learning and academic achievement: An overview and analysis. In B. J. Zimmerman & D. H. Schunk (Eds.), *Self-regulated learning and academic achievement: Theoretical perspectives* (2nd ed., pp. 1–38). Mahwah, NJ: Erlbaum.

Zimmerman, B. J., Bandura, A., & Martinez-Pons, M. (1992). Self-motivation for academic attainment: The role of self-efficacy beliefs and personal goal setting. *American Educational Research Journal, 29*(3), 663–676.

Index

A

ability grouping, 32–33
academic behaviors, 75–78
Accountability in Action (Reeves), 19
active learning, 40, 47–48, 56, 164
    best practices, 49–50
    educational practices, 48–49
    facilitated approaches, 50, 53–55
    improving student learning, 50–55
    instruction and inquiry balance, 50, 52
    let students do the talking, 50–52
    promoting, 9–10
    student-friendly environments, 50
affective dispositions, 19
Aldip, A., 64–66
Allington, R., 7, 34
alternative scheduling, 41
argument-driven inquiry, 54
The Art and Science of Teaching (Marzano), 17
assessment
    assessing, 100–102
    buffer times, 68
    considering preassessment, 102
    embracing as learning, 103
    feedback and, 95–106
    for and as learning, 95
    formative, 60–61, 131
    learning target trackers, 64–66
    multiple-choice, 12
    of learning, 60
    reassessment opportunities, 103–104
    self-, 11, 84
    summative, 97
Ausubel, D., 95, 97–98

B

back-to-school nights, 139
balancing instruction and empowerment, 153–154
Behavior (Weber), 73, 83–84, 126
behavioral skills, 40, 88, 164
    believing educators can motivate students, 89–91
    best practices, 75–80
    educational practices, 74–75
    empowerment mindset equation, 85–89
    encouraging students to take responsibility for learning, 103
    improving student learning, 80–91
    nurturing, 10–11, 73–74
    six steps to develop behavioral skills, 80–85
believing in educators to motivate students, 80, 89–91
belonging, 74–75, 77, 82, 86, 142
best practices, 3, 8
    active learning, 49–50
    emphasizing skills, 111–116
    empowering parents, 139–142
    learning targets, 60–61
    nurturing motivation, 75–80
    predicting and preventing challenges, 33–34
    rigorous learning, 126–128
    staff engagement, 151–152
    teaching less, 17–20
    two-way feedback, 11, 95, 99–106, 164
Beyranevand, M., 104–105
Black, P., 11, 60
Blackburn, B., 12, 127

Blanchard, K., 151
Bloom, B., 5, 9–11, 32, 34, 41–42, 61, 67, 97
    taxonomy of educational objectives, 115–116
Boaler, J., 132–133
Boothe, D., 150
Bourassa, M., 132
Brookings Institution
    research on skills learning, 112–113
buffer times, 41–42, 62, 67–68
Buffum, A., 34
Bulach, C., 150

C

categories of depth, 127
challenges
    planning for/mitigating, 155–156
    predicting/preventing, 31–43
Chappuis, J., 59–60
Chicago Public Schools, 8
City, E., 3, 12, 126–127
claims-evidence-reasoning model, 119
class differences, 2, 145
Classroom Assessment (Popham), 18
cognitive self-regulation, 77
Cohen, D., 151
Cohen, G., 11, 78–79
collaborative leadership, 149–161
collaborative learning, 41, 48–49, 50
    environment for, 129–130
collaborative teaching, 6, 20–23, 33–34, 99–100
collective responsibility, 6, 21, 33–34
collective teacher efficacy, 89–91
College, Career, and Civic Life Framework for Social Studies State Standards, 115, 143
Collins, J., 13, 152
Comer School Development Program, 141–142
Comer, J., 13
Common Core State Standards, 16, 18, 22
    English language arts, 114, 154
    mathematics, 114, 154
common formative assessments, 131
common learning experiences, 131–133

compliance mandates, 5
comprehension strategies, 7, 45
Conley, D.
    research on skills learning, 112
continuous improvement, 21, 25–27
cooperative learning, 50, 73
Costa, A., 128
course repetition, 33
creating a culture of growth, 158–159
cultural diversity, 145
curriculum
    behavioral, 88
    depth over breadth, 117–118
    emphasizing skills, 109–121
    guaranteed and viable, 15–17
    intended, 17
    learned, 17
    maps, 9, 17, 110

D

Daggett, B., 12, 49
Danielson, C., 9, 49
Deming, D., 79
Deming, W. E., 152
Depth of Knowledge model (Webb), 116
depth over breadth, 117–118
Dickson, M., 118
differentiated supports, 105–106
Differentiation and the Brain (Sousa & Tomlinson), 49
differentiation, 40, 52, 84–85
direct instruction vs. inquiry, 52
Donavan, K., 131–132
dot grading, 103
dream statements, 26
Drucker, P., 152
Duckworth, A., 11, 75
DuFour, Rebecca, 10
DuFour, Richard, 1, 5–6, 10–11, 17, 152
Dweck, C., 11, 75, 78–79

E

Eaker, R., 10, 152
Economist Group
    research on employee attributes, 112

educational practices, 3, 8
    active learning, 48–49
    emphasizing skills, 110
    empowering parents, 137–139
    learning targets, 60
    nurturing motivation, 74–75
    predicting and preventing challenges, 32–33
    rigorous learning, 125–126
    staff engagement, 149–151
    teaching less, 16–17
    two-way feedback, 11, 95, 99–106, 164
effecting change, 7–8
effective schools movement, 139–140
Elmore, R., 3, 12, 126–127
Embedded Formative Assessment (Wiliam), 61
emphasizing skills, 11–12, 109, 120–121, 164
    best practices, 111–116
    claims-evidence-reasoning model, 119
    depth over breadth, 117–118
    educational practices, 110
    emphasizing inquiry, 120
    evolving homework practices, 119
    improving student learning, 116–120
    modeling understanding, 120
    prioritizing skills learning, 118–119
Empower (Spencer & Juliani), 49
empowering educators, 21–22, 160–161
    balancing instruction and empowerment, 153–154
    best practices, 151–152
    creating a culture of growth, 158–159
    educational practices, 149–151
    establishing trust, 154–155
    improving student learning, 152–160
    leaning in, 156
    learning to lead, 156–158
    planning for challenges, 155–156
    sharing/developing leadership skills, 159–160
empowering parents, 12–13, 133, 145–146, 164
    best practices, 139–142
    educational practices, 137–139
    improving student learning, 142–145
    including parents as interventionists, 144–145
    making common sense more common, 145
    surveying and responding to parent needs, 143–144
    ten educational commandments for parents, 143
empowering students, 102
empowerment mindset equation, 80, 85–89
Engaging Students with Poverty in Mind (Jensen), 140–141
English-language learners, 2
    parents of, 145
    scaffolding and, 23
environmental obstacles, 78
environments
    for collaborative learning, 129–130
    rigor-friendly, 129–130
    seating arrangements, 48–50, 129–130
    student-friendly, 50
Erkens, C., 99–101
establishing trust with staff, 154–155
exam wrappers, 11

F

facilitated approaches, 50, 53–55
Farrington, C., 11, 75
fatigue. *See* initiative fatigue
feedback
    best practices, 97–99
    educational practices, 96–97
    finding time for, 99–100, 105
    from parents, 138
    improving student learning, 99–106
    passing upward, 105–106
    two-way, 11, 95, 99–106, 164
Fiarman, S., 3, 12, 126–127
Fisher, D., 51, 56
five E lesson design, 53, 55
fluency, 7, 45, 81
Focus (Schmoker), 18
formative assessment, 60–61, 131
fostering learning, 3
four corners, 50
four Cs, 50
Frey, N., 51, 56
Fullan, M., 5–6, 13, 98, 140, 143–144

G

Garden Grove Unified School District, 20
    parent partnership, 143–144
good mistakes, 86–87
Google
    research on employee attributes, 112
grade retention, 33
grading, 95–96
    highlight, 103
graduation rates, 1
guaranteed and viable curriculum, 15–17
Guskey, T., 34, 97

H

habits of mind, 128
Hamilton Project
    research on skills learning, 112–113
Hattie, J., 11, 75, 89, 98, 163–164
The Heart of Change (Kotter & Cohen), 151
Heath, C., 13, 152
Heath, D., 13, 152
Heritage Computer Science Academy (Garden Grove, Calif.), 8, 144
Hiebert, J., 61
Hierck, T., 34
highlight grading, 103
Holmes, C., 21, 24–26
homework
    lagging, 119
    parents and, 138
hopelessness, 84
How People Learn (National Research Council), 49
Hyde, Karajean, 21–22

I

icons of complexity, 127–128
immediate supports, 40–41
implemented curricula, 17
improving student learning
    active learning, 50–55
    addressing standardized testing, 23–24
    alternative scheduling, 41
    assessing assessments, 100–102
    balancing instruction and empowerment, 153–154
    believing educators can motivate students, 89–91
    buffer times, 41–42, 67–68
    choosing priority standards, 21–23
    claims-evidence-reasoning model, 119
    collaborative classes, 41
    considering preassessments, 102
    continuous improvement, 25–27
    creating a culture of growth, 158–159
    depth over breadth, 117–118
    embracing assessment as learning, 102
    emphasizing inquiry, 120
    emphasizing skills, 116–120
    empowering parents, 142–145
    empowerment mindset equation, 85–89
    establishing trust, 154–155
    evolving homework practices, 119
    facilitated approaches, 50, 53–55
    finding time for feedback, 99–100, 105
    including parents as interventionists, 144–145
    increasing rigor of tasks, 130–133
    instruction and inquiry balance, 50, 52
    integrating RTI with PLC, 42–43
    leaning in, 156
    learning targets, 62–66
    learning to lead, 156–158
    let students do the talking, 50–52
    making common sense more common, 145
    modeling understanding, 120
    nurturing motivation, 80–91
    passing feedback upward, 105–106
    planning backward, 66–67
    planning for challenges, 155–156
    predicting and preventing challenges, 34–43
    prioritizing skills learning, 118–119
    prioritizing standards, 21, 24
    providing support immediately, 40–41
    reassessment opportunities, 103–104
    rigor-friendly learning environment, 129–130
    rigorous learning, 129–133

scaffolding, 23
sharing/developing leadership skills, 159–160
six steps to develop behavioral skills, 80–85
staff engagement, 152–160
student responsibility for learning, 103
student-friendly environments, 50
surveying and responding to parent needs, 143–144
teaching less, 20–21, 39–40
ten educational commandments for parents, 143
two-way feedback, 99–106
using RTI, 34–39

In Praise of American Educators (DuFour), 1, 17
including parents as interventionists, 143–145
initiative fatigue, 4–5, 7
inquiry
    argument-driven, 54
    balancing with instruction, 50, 52
    emphasizing, 120
    vs. direct instruction, 52
inquiry-based approach to learning, 10, 53–54
Instructional Rounds in Education (City et al.), 126–127
intended curricula, 17
Irvine Unified School District (Calif.), 4–5, 19, 21–22, 25, 35–36, 39–42, 47–48, 50–51, 62, 64, 67, 79–80, 85, 101–106, 115–120, 129–133, 137, 152–160
    Parent Education Program, 145

J

Jensen, E., 13, 140–141
Jetzer, A., 160
jigsaw, 50
Johnson, S., 151
Juliani, A. J., 10, 49

K

Kagan, S., 49
Kallick, B., 128
Kaplan, S., 127–128
Khan Academy, 104–105
Kotter, J., 151
Krebs, C., 79, 84

L

labeling, 10–11, 16, 32–33, 74, 89–91
lagging homework, 119
Latino Educational Attainment Initiatives, 143
leadership practices, 8, 164
    active learning, 9–10
    balancing instruction and empowerment, 153–154
    best practices, 151–152
    categories of mistakes, 150–151
    creating a culture of growth, 158–159
    emphasizing skills, 11–12
    empowering parents, 12–13
    establishing trust, 154–155
    inspiring staff engagement, 13
    leader as coach, 152
    leaning in, 156
    learning to lead, 156–158
    nurturing motivation, 10–11
    planning for challenges, 155–156
    predicting and preventing challenges, 9
    promoting rigorous learning, 12
    sharing/developing leadership skills, 159–160
    styles, 149–150
    teaching less, 9
    two-way feedback, 11, 95, 99–106, 164
    using learning targets, 10
leaning in, 156
learned curricula, 17
Learning by Doing (DuFour et al.), 6
learning disabilities, 32–33
learning environments. *See* environments
The Learning Leader (Reeves), 19
learning strategies, 75–77
learning target trackers, 64–66, 89, 102
    sample, 65
learning targets, 10, 59, 68–69, 164
    best practices, 60–61
    buffer times, 67–68
    creating, 62–64
    defined, 63
    educational practices, 60
    improving student learning, 62–68
    planning backward, 66–67
    tracking, 64–66, 89, 102

learning to lead, 156–158
Leonard, A., 36–37, 42
Leong, M., 129–131
let students do the talking, 50–52
Lezotte, L., 10, 13, 75
lines of communication, 50
Looney, S., 131

M

Machesky, S., 153–154, 156, 160–161
MacKenzie, T., 10, 49
making common sense more common, 143, 145
Making Standards Work (Reeves), 19
Many, T., 10
Marzano, R., 9–10, 15, 17, 49, 61
mastery learning, 61
Mattos, M., 10, 34
Maxwell, J., 13, 151
McTighe, J., 9–10, 19
Medina, M., 144–145
meet and greets, 145
memorization vs. thinking, 11–12, 110
mindsets, 75–77
Ministry of Education of Singapore, 19
Mischel, R., 79
modeling
　skills, 83–84, 90
　understanding, 120
Morris, A., 61
Motion Leadership (Fullan), 5
Motivation. *See* nurturing motivation
Muhammad, A., 13, 141
multiple-choice assessments, 12
multisensory awareness, 45
multitiered system of supports. *See* response to intervention
My Favorite No, 87

N

A Nation at Risk (National Commission on Excellence in Education), 120
National Assessment of Educational Progress, 1
National Mathematics Advisory Panel, 75
National Reading Panel, 7–8, 75
National Research Council, 10, 49, 118

The New Meaning of Educational Change (Fullan), 140
Next Generation Science Standards, 55, 114, 154
Northwood High School (Irvine, Calif.), 51, 118
note taking, 73, 82
nurturing motivation, 10–11, 73–74
　believing educators can motivate students, 89-91
　best practices, 75–80
　educational practices, 74–75
　empowerment mindset equation, 85-89
　improving student learning, 80–91
　six steps to developing student behavioral skills, 80-85

O

The One Minute Manager (Blanchard & Johnson), 151
open houses, 139
open middle, 132
Orange County Business Council, 143
Organisation for Economic Co-operation and Development (OECD), 1
　Programme for International Student Assessment, 1–2
organization skills, 73, 81–82
　modeling, 83–84

P

pacing guides, 9, 17, 110
parents. *See* empowering parents
Parham, C., 106
Partnership for 21st Century Learning
　research on future-ready skills, 111
passive learning, 9–10
　vs. active learning, 47–48, 50
Pehrson, J., 88, 158
perseverance, 73, 75–77
Phillips, H., 62–64
phonemic awareness skills, 7, 45
phonics skills, 7, 45, 81
Pickett, W., 150
Pinchot, M., 13, 143–144
planning backward, 62, 66–67
planning for challenges, 155–156

planning skills, 81–82
    modeling, 83–84
PLC at Work, 4–6, 9, 11, 15, 36, 62, 96–97, 100, 152, 159–160, 163–164
    integrating RTI with, 42–43
    prioritizing standards through, 21, 24
Polls of the Public's Attitudes Toward the Public School, 1
Popham, W. J., 18–19
Portola High School (Irvine, Calif.), 88, 117
poverty, 1–2, 78, 140–141
power standards, 19
preassessments, 102
predicting and preventing challenges, 9, 31, 164
    alternative scheduling, 41
    best practices, 33–34
    buffer times, 41–42
    collaborative classes, 41
    educational practices, 32–33
    improving student learning, 34–43
    integrating RTI with PLC, 42–43
    providing support immediately, 40–41
    using RTI, 34–39
prioritizing standards, 17–20
    choosing, 21–23
    through PLC at Work, 21, 24
professional learning communities. *See* PLC at Work
Programme for International Student Assessment (PISA), 19
project-based learning, 130–133
punishment, 74

Q

question formulation technique (Rothstein & Santana), 52, 55

R

reading levels, 7–8, 45
reassessment, 103–105
Reeves, D., 5, 9, 19
Resendez, J., 117–118, 120–121
respecting student readiness, 84–85
response to intervention, 9, 24, 31, 33–34, 90
    behavioral, 85
    defined, 34–35
    integrating with PLC, 42–43
    Tier 1, 35–37
    Tier 2, 37–38
    Tier 3, 38–39
Results (Schmoker), 18
retention, 12
Richard Henry Dana Elementary School (Capistrano Unified School District), 8, 157
Rigor in Your Classroom (Blackburn), 127
Rigor/Relevance Framework (Daggett), 49
rigorous learning, 12, 164
    best practices, 126–128
    defined, 127
    educational practices, 125–126
    improving student learning, 129–133
    increasing rigor of tasks, 130–133
    learning environment, 129–130
Russell, M., 35

S

Saffel Street Elementary School (Lawrenceburg, Kan.), 88–89
Same but Different Math (Looney), 131
same-but-different tasks, 131–133
scaffolding, 10, 20, 23, 74, 105–106
Schmoker, M., 9, 18
Schneider, L., 51
seating arrangements, 48–50, 129–130
self-advocacy, 73
self-assessment, 11, 84
self-efficacy, 142
self-regulation, 49, 79, 82
    cognitive, 76–77
    modeling, 83–84
Senge, P., 152
seven correlates of effectives schools, 139–140
shaming in blaming, 138
sharing/developing leadership skills, 159–160
Sinek, S., 13, 151
six steps to developing student behavioral skills, 80-85
    define/make sense of skills, 80, 82-83
    differentiate supports, 80, 84-85
    identify most critical skills, 80, 81-82

intervene appropriately, 80, 84-85
measure student success, 80, 84
model skills, 80, 83-84
skills learning, 118–119
skills. See emphasizing skills
Slavin, R., 34
Smith, C., 151
Snyder, K. M., 10, 13, 75
social learning, 50
social skills, 75–77, 82
    modeling, 83–84
Sousa, D., 49
special needs, 20, 23, 32–33, 45
Spencer, J., 10, 49
spiral reviews, 119
Spitzer, S., 61
staff engagement, 13, 160–161, 164
    balancing instruction and empowerment, 153–154
    best practices, 151–152
    creating a culture of growth, 158–159
    educational practices, 149–151
    establishing trust, 154–155
    improving student learning, 152–160
    leaning in, 156
    learning to lead, 156–158
    planning for challenges, 155–156
    sharing/developing leadership skills, 159–160
staff turnover, 151
stakeholders and leadership, 154–157
standardized testing, 110
    addressing, 20, 23–24
start with why, 151
start-doing plans, 4
Stewart, L., 64–66, 68
Stiggins, R., 10–11, 59
stop-doing plans, 4
student engagement, 49–50, 59
    buffer times, 67–68
student responsibility for learning, 103
student-friendly environments, 50
summative assessment, 97

surveying and responding to parent needs, 142–144
Switch (Heath & Heath), 152

T

Talman Elementary School (Chicago, Ill.), 144–145
task predicts performance principle, 126–127
Tate, M., 126
Teach Less, Learn More initiative, 20–21, 25, 130, 164
Teach Math Like This, Not Like That (Beyranevand), 104
teacher-as-facilitator, 10
teacher-student relations, 1, 11
    behavioral skills, 85–86
teaching less, 9, 15–16
    addressing standardized testing, 23–24
    best practices, 17–20
    choosing priority standards, 21–23
    continuous improvement, 25–27
    educational practices, 3, 8, 16–17
    improving student learning, 20–27, 39–40
    prioritizing standards, 21, 24
    scaffolding, 23
teaching to the test, 66–67
Teaching with Poverty in Mind (Jensen), 140–141
Teitel, L., 3, 12, 126–127
ten educational commandments for parents, 142–143
Texas Essential Knowledge and Skills, 154
think-pair-share, 50
time management skills, 81–82
    modeling, 83–84
Timperley, H., 11, 98
Tomlinson, C. A., 49
Transformative Assessment (Popham), 18
Trends in International Mathematics and Science Studies, 1, 19
Tuominen, K., 157, 159–160
two-way feedback, 11, 164
    assessing assessments, 100–102
    considering preassessments, 102

embracing assessment as learning, 102
finding time for feedback, 99–100, 105
passing feedback upward, 105–106
reassessment opportunities, 103–104
student responsibility for learning, 103

U

Understanding by Design (Wiggins & McTighe), 19

V

Visible Learning, 34
vocabulary, 7, 81
Vygotsky, L., 9, 49, 98

W

wait to fail model, 9

Walton, G., 11, 78–79
Webb, N., 116
Welch, J., 151
What Works in Schools (Marzano), 17
Which One Doesn't Belong? (Bourassa), 132
Wiggins, G., 9–10, 19
Wiliam, D., 10–11, 60–61
Woodbridge High School (Irvine, Calif.), 52, 131
work stations, 129–130
worksheets, 126

Y

years at a glance, 26–27

Z

Zimmerman, B., 11, 49, 61, 75

Behavior: The Forgotten Curriculum
Chris Weber
Discover how to fully prepare students for college, careers, and life by nurturing their behavioral skills along with their academic skills. Learn how to employ the most effective behavioral-skill exercises for your particular class and form unique relationships with every learner.
BKF828

Leading Modern Learning, Second Edition
Jay McTighe and Greg Curtis
Redesign education for 21st century learners with the support of *Leading Modern Learning*. More than a simple refresh, the latest edition outlines a reworked blueprint for major education reform and incorporates new insights, experiences, and tools for implementing modern learning practices.
BKF850

Swimming in the Deep End
Jennifer Abrams
Acquire the knowledge and resources necessary to lead successful change initiatives in schools. In *Swimming in the Deep End*, author Jennifer Abrams dives deep into the four foundational skills required of effective leadership and provides ample guidance for cultivating each.
BKF830

Time for Change
Anthony Muhammad and Luis F. Cruz
Exceptional leaders have four distinctive skills: strong communication, the ability to build trust, the ability to increase the skills of those they lead, and a results orientation. *Time for Change* offers powerful guidance for those seeking to develop and strengthen these skills.
BKF683

Solution Tree | Press
a division of Solution Tree

Visit SolutionTree.com or call 800.733.6786 to order.

GLOBAL PD

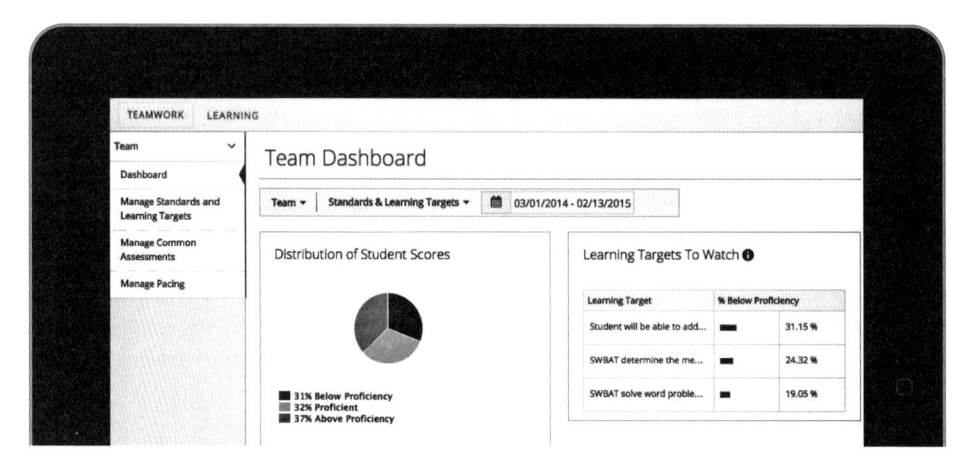

The **Power to Improve** Is in Your Hands

Global PD gives educators focused and goals-oriented training from top experts. You can rely on this innovative online tool to improve instruction in every classroom.

- Get unlimited, on-demand access to guided video and book content from top Solution Tree authors.

- Improve practices with personalized virtual coaching from PLC-certified trainers.

- Customize learning based on skill level and time commitments.

▶ **REQUEST A FREE DEMO TODAY**
SolutionTree.com/GlobalPD

Solution Tree